Borderline Personality Disorder

A Guide to Help You Learn About Everything You Need To Know To Live With Borderline Personality Disorder

MELINDA QUINN

TABLE OF CONTENTS

02

04

05

LIVING WITH BORDERLINE PERSONALITY DISORDER
129

07

SELF-CARE FOR PEOPLE WITH BPD
172

08

09

TRANSFERENCE-FOCUSED THERAPY AND SCHEMA-FOCUSED THERAPY
226

10

Introduction

A borderline personality disorder is a difficult disease to diagnose and treat. It has an impact on how a person perceives himself and other people. Genes, cognitive impairments, or environmental variables all have the potential to contribute to borderline personality disorder. Because of the broad range of potential risk factors, it is difficult to predict who will be affected by the disease. It is characterized by strong emotions and relationships and feelings of insecurity and self-doubt, among other symptoms. Everything in a person's life seems unstable when they have it, including their emotions, thoughts, behavior, relationships, and, in some cases, their identity. People suffering from this disorder have characterized it as the sensation of having an exposed nerve ending, which leaves them vulnerable to being quickly triggered by little things. However, there are effective therapies available for this disease. People who have this personality disorder often experience a great deal of emotional instability. In addition, it affects a person's self-image, preferences, and aspirations. This often causes individuals to get disoriented in their sense of self. It is difficult for a person to feel comfortable in their skin due to the disorder. Because of their high levels of anguish and resentment, individuals are susceptible to being quickly offended. They struggle with their own and other people's perceptions of themselves and others, which may create pain in a variety of aspects of their life. People who have it experience acute anxiety of instability and abandonment. As a consequence, individuals have difficulty being by themselves. Aggression, mood changes, and impulsive behavior are other characteristics of the disease. These characteristics may cause individuals to avoid being in the company of someone suffering from this disorder. On top of that, many individuals who suffer from the disease have difficulty understanding themselves and how others understand them. As a result, they are very sensitive. It is a disease that affects both the mind and the body. Its signs begin to emerge throughout the early adolescent years and progressively improve as they age into middle age and beyond. Most individuals suffering from it behave impulsively, feel strong emotions, and suffer from detachment and psychosis when they are most disturbed. Relationship problems may arise as a result of this emotional instability. Aside from that, the incapacity to self-soothe may result in impulsive and risky conduct. In this book, you'll find more detail about this topic.

01

Understanding Borderline Personality Disorder

A borderline personality disorder is a psychological disease that affects both men and women. When it first occurs, it is typically  around adolescence or early adulthood. People who have this personality disorder have severe mood fluctuations, weak relationships, and difficulty regulating their emotions. They have a greater risk of suicide and self-destructive conduct than the general population. Symptoms usually diminish with time, and therapy and medication may be beneficial.

1.1 What is a Borderline Personality Disorder and how does it manifest itself?

It is a severe mental disease that affects both men and women. People with this personality disorder have difficulty managing their emotions, controlling their conduct, and establishing stable relationships. They participate in hazardous or destructive conduct, such as irresponsible driving or unsafe sex, are more likely to be arrested. If you have this disorder, you may have strong emotions that shift abruptly and the desire to hurt yourself. To treat it it's used a combination of Psychotherapy and medication.

Adolescence or early adulthood are the most common ages for the onset of BPD symptoms. They may grow less severe with time. Known as manic-depressive sickness, this disorder is a mental condition that causes individuals to experience periods of extreme high and low emotions. People suffering from this disease experience moments of being excessively happy and cheerful or irritated and intervals of being very depressed or feeling normal. The disease is called borderline disorder because of the extremes of highs and lows or two poles of mood.

On the other hand, patients' emotions may not always follow a cyclic pattern, and they may experience both highs and lows simultaneously. The occurrence of a manic episode is the distinguishing feature of this disease. Throughout reality, to fulfill the criteria for borderline illness, individuals must have had at least one manic episode in their lives, whether or not they have also had a depressive episode at any point.

Hypomania or mania refers to periods when a person is excessively enthusiastic and confident in their abilities. Confusion, irritation, anger, and even fury may rapidly develop as a result of these emotions.

The term depressive describes a person's feelings of sadness or depression at these times. Because borderline depression and major depression symptoms are so similar, individuals with borderline disorder's depression are often misdiagnosed as having major depression. This is why it is so critical to do a thorough mania screening. The majority of people who suffer from this mental illness spend three times as much time in depressive periods as in manic episodes.

1.2 Factors causing Borderline Personality Disorder

According to healthcare professionals, this personality disorder is caused by a mix of genetic and environmental variables, including:

- Having been sexually, emotionally, or physically abused.

- The neglect, abuse, or separation from a parent.

- Having a family history of borderline personality disorder.

- Having communication problems between the areas of the brain that regulate mood and behavior.

It has been shown that people with this personality disorder have differences in their brain structure and function, particularly in the parts of their brain that regulate impulse control and emotion regulation. Individuals with this disorder have evidence of differences in their brain structure and function. However, it is yet unknown if these changes are a consequence of having it or whether they contribute to the disorder's development.

Many individuals diagnosed with this disorder have had negative childhood experiences such as abuse, trauma, or neglect and being removed from their caregivers at a young age. However, not all individuals with it experienced one of these childhood events, and many people who have had them do not develop the disorder.

Psychiatrists generally agree that it is caused by a mix of inherited or internal biological elements and external environmental variables, such as traumatic events throughout infancy. Many complicated processes are going on in the brain of someone who has this personality disorder, and experts are still trying to figure out what they all imply. To put it another way, if you have it, your brain is always on high alert. Things seem to be more frightening and stressful to you than they do to other people. Because it is so readily tripped, the fight-or-flight switch may take over your logical brain, activating primal survival impulses that are not always suitable for the circumstances at hand. It may seem that there is nothing you can do in this situation.

After all, what can you do if your brain isn't the same as everyone else's? However, the reality is that you can alter your brain. Creating new neural pathways occurs every time you practice a new coping response or self-soothing method, which you should do every day. Some therapies, such as mindfulness meditation, have increased the amount of brain matter in the patient's brain. And the more you practice, the stronger and more automatic these neural connections will become as you progress. Don't give up, then! You can alter your thoughts, feelings, and actions if you put in the effort.

Personality disorders and Social stigmatization

When we speak about personality in psychology, we're talking to the distinctive patterns of thinking, feeling, and acting that distinguish each of us from others. Although no one behaves precisely in the same manner, we tend to interact with and connect with the environment in pretty constant ways. As a result, individuals are often characterized as shy, meticulous or fun-loving, and other such adjectives. These are characteristics of a person's personality.

Given how closely personality and identity are intertwined, hearing the phrase personality disorder may make you feel like something is fundamentally wrong with who you are. This disorder, on the other hand, is not a character judgment. According to clinical definitions, having it implies that your way of connecting to the world is substantially different from the average individual. This leads you to have persistent difficulties in various aspects of your life, including your relationships, job, and emotions about yourself and other people.

1.3 Signs and Symptoms of BPD

This personality disorder presents itself in various ways, but mental health experts categorize the symptoms into nine main categories for diagnosis. At least five of these symptoms must be present for you to be diagnosed with this disorder. Furthermore, the symptoms must have been present for a lengthy period, often starting in puberty and affect many aspects of your life.

The fear of being abandoned.

People with this personality disorder are often afraid of being abandoned or left alone. Even seemingly harmless events such as a loved one coming home late from work or leaving for the weekend may cause tremendous anxiety. When this happens, it is common for people to make frantic attempts to keep the other person near. You may plead, cling to your loved ones, create arguments, monitor their whereabouts, or even physically prevent them from going. Unfortunately, this kind of conduct tends to have the opposite impact, i.e., it alienates people.

Having unstable relationships.

People who have this personality disorder have relationships that are passionate yet short-lived. It's possible to fall in love fast, thinking that each new person would be the one who will make you feel whole, only to be swiftly let down by them. Your relationships seem to be either great or terrible, with little room for a happy medium. As a consequence of your quick swings from idealization to devaluation, rage, and hatred, your lovers, friends, and family members may also experience emotional whiplash.

An ambiguous or changing sense of self.

When you have it, your sense of self is usually unstable. You may have positive feelings about yourself at times, but you may also despise yourself or even consider yourself to be wicked at other times. You most likely have no clear sense of who you are or what you want to accomplish with your life. Consequently, you may find yourself changing professions, acquaintances, loves, religion, beliefs, ambitions, and even your sexual orientation regularly.

Self-destructive and impulsive actions.

If you have this disorder, you may engage in hazardous, sensation-seeking activities, particularly when distressed. You may spend money you can't afford on impulse, overindulge in food, drive recklessly, shoplift, engage in hazardous sexual behavior, or overindulge in drugs or alcoholic beverages. These hazardous habits may make you feel better in the short term, but they are detrimental to your health and the health of others around you in the long run.

Self-harm

Suicidal ideation and intentional self-harm are prevalent among individuals who have this personality disorder. Suicidal conduct involves:

- Having suicidal thoughts.

- Making suicidal gestures or threats.

- Attempting to commit suicide in some way or another.

Self-harm includes any efforts to injure oneself that are not motivated by suicidal thoughts. Cutting and burning are two of the most common types of self-harm.

Extreme emotional ups and downs.

Unstable emotions and moods are prevalent among those suffering from it. You may be joyful one minute and depressed the next. It happens to everyone. Little things that other people don't seem to notice may throw you into a spiral of mental turmoil. Even while these mood swings are strong, they tend to dissipate rather quickly, in contrast to the emotional swings associated with depression or mental illness, typically lasting just a few minutes or hours.

Persistent feelings of emptiness.

People who have a personality disorder often describe feeling empty, as if there is a hole or a vacuum within them. You may feel as if you are nothing or nobody if you are experiencing severe low self-esteem. Because this sensation is unpleasant, you may attempt to fill the vacuum with substances such as drugs, food or sex. Nothing, on the other hand, is gratifying.

Anger erupts violently.

If you have a borderline personality disorder, you may battle with strong anger and a quick temper. You may also have difficulty regulating your emotions after the fuse has been lit, screaming, throwing objects, or being overtaken by anger. The fact that this rage is not always aimed inwards should not be overlooked. You may spend a significant amount of time feeling resentful of yourself.

Having a suspicious or out-of-touch feeling with reality.

People who have it often experience paranoia or suspicious thoughts about the intentions of others. When you are under stress, you may even lose contact with reality, referred to as dissociation in the medical community. You may feel hazy, spaced out, or as if you're not in your own body. It is not always the case that shifting mood states follow a predictable pattern, and sadness does not always occur in conjunction with manic periods. It is also possible for a person to experience the same mood state many times before experiencing the opposing emotion.

Mood Swings.

Mood shifts can occur over few weeks to many months or even several years. It is critical to recognize that the person's mood shifts depart from his or her normal self and that the mood change is maintained for an extended time. The duration of mania may last for many days or weeks, whereas depression can last for several weeks or months. Even though shorter bouts of mania or depression may indicate more severe episodes in the future, they are often insufficient to identify a person with this mental illness.

It is possible to have various degrees of intensity in the depressed and manic phases depending on who you are and when you are experiencing them.
• Sadness
• Irritability
• Loss of energy
• Restlessness
• Sleep disorders
• Difficulty concentrating
• A change in appetite
• Poor concentration
• Increased sex drive
• Excessive crying
• Difficulty making choices

• Extreme happiness and excitement.
• Feelings of worthlessness or hopelessness.
• Loss of enjoyment from once pleasurable things.
• Sudden changes from being happy to be irritable or angry.

Some individuals may develop psychosis, in which they see and hear things that aren't there and retain erroneous ideas that they are unable to dispel on their own. In certain cases, people believe they possess superhuman abilities and capabilities or are god-like in their beliefs and actions. Patients suffering from depression may also have psychosis, in which they hear voices or have delusions.

1.4 BPD and Associated Disorders

Effective treatment must take into consideration associated diseases. Many individuals who are diagnosed with a borderline personality disorder also suffer from co-occurring disorders, such as:

- Depression

- Eating disorders

- Anxiety disorders

- Psychological disorders

- Post-traumatic stress disorder

- Substance abuse disorder

1.5 Myths about Borderline Personality Disorder

There are a lot of misconceptions about this disorder. Some mental health professionals, as well as the general public, are misinformed about this illness. This ambiguity may affect and affect the way that individuals are treated. Even worse, long-standing misconceptions about the illness may prevent individuals from seeking treatment for it, particularly if they believe others are misinterpreting their experience. The following are some popular myths and misconceptions:

Myth: It is incurable and thus untreatable.

A borderline personality disorder is a very durable condition. Historically, since it is impacted someone's personality, many people were quick to infer that it was untreatable because someone's personality cannot be altered. Many therapies, including dialectical behavior therapy, transference-focused psychotherapy and mentalization-based treatment, have lately been shown to be successful as treatments. General psychiatric management, a less intense strategy that is becoming more popular throughout the globe, is one of the techniques being used more often.

Its diagnosis does not imply that a person will be plagued by symptoms for the rest of their lives. Symptoms fluctuate in intensity and frequency as a result of therapy. It is possible for many individuals who have the disease to have productive lives.

Myth: People suffering from this disorder are victims of child abuse.

The truth is that this is not always the case. While some instances of borderline personality disorder are caused by childhood trauma, it is more probable that a diagnosis is the consequence of a mix of contextual variables rather than one single one. Attachment, early trauma, biological variables, and societal factors are all examples of risk factors.

Myth: It is just a problem for women.

It is estimated that approximately 13 million people in the US have this personality disorder. Previously thought to be more prevalent in women, the biggest research ever conducted on mental illnesses has shown that it affects men and women equally. One possible reason it seems to impact more women than men is that women are more likely than males to seek mental health treatment. Because research on borderline personality disorder is often performed in a psychiatric environment, males with borderline personality disorder were historically less likely to be included in these research initiatives. The fact that it is often misdiagnosed in males is another reason. Many males who suffer from the disease are also diagnosed with depression or post-traumatic stress disorder.

1.6 What is the Procedure for Diagnosing Borderline Personality Disorder?

A diagnosis of this illness may only be established after a thorough examination of the patient's symptoms, including their severity, duration, and frequency. Periods of hypomania or mania are the most striking signs of BPD. Obtaining a detailed history from close friends and family members may be very helpful in distinguishing this mental illness from severe depression. If you or someone you know is experiencing signs of BPD, you should see your primary care physician or a psychiatrist. A referral to a mental health professional who is suitable for the situation may then be made.

It is necessary to do a comprehensive medical examination. Your physician may likely inquire about your personal and family history of mental illness. In addition, you may be requested to complete a questionnaire for screening for mood disorders or depression. This is a series of questions to which you will be required to respond either orally or in writing, depending on your preference.

Individuals with this personality disorder are diagnosed by assessing their symptoms and checking their medical history. A doctor may also perform an examination and laboratory testing to rule out any medical conditions contributing to the symptoms.

A person must exhibit the following symptoms in a range of settings to diagnose them.
• Impulsive actions
• Emotional instability
• Feelings of emptiness
• Inappropriate and strong rage

• Disruptions in one's sense of self
• Transient paranoid or dissociative symptoms.
• Interpersonal connections that are unstable.
• Behaviors such as suicidal or self-harming thoughts or actions
In addition, a doctor or therapist will rule out any mental health problems that may be causing the same symptoms. This category includes:
• Bipolar disorder
• Histrionic personality disorder
• Narcissistic personality disorder

1.7 Identification of Borderline Personality Disorder in Oneself or Others

People who have this personality disorder have difficulty with self-regulation. Personal self-regulation is the capacity to control one's emotions, thoughts. And actions in ways that result in favorable results, including high levels of confidence and healthy relationships. To be formally diagnosed, a person must show five or more symptoms linked to the condition. These symptoms must be persistent and affect many areas of one's life. There are just a few signs of this personality disorder that medical professionals recognize.

Relationship Instability.

People suffering from it are prone to have intense and short-lived relationships. It is extremely typical for someone suffering from this condition to have passionate, unstable relationships filled with dramatic and rapidly shifting emotions. It is possible for someone suffering from it to fall in love fast and believe that others would make them happy. Typically, this leaves the individual feeling wounded and disappointed, and it may exacerbate already severe mood swings even more. It is possible for individuals suffering from this disease to have either ideal or terrible relationships, with quick shifts in perspective coming from feelings of rage, resentment, and devaluation.

Extreme Emotional Ups and Downs.

A person suffering from this disease is prone to having unpredictable moods and emotions. The seemingly little things that others take for granted, such as someone not holding the door open for you or making a new friend, can be very thrilling or irritating, depending on your perspective. The moods of many people suffering from this disease may swing from joyful to very unhappy or dissatisfied in an instant. Their emotions are also very strong, and their timing is completely unexpected. The duration of these attacks may range from a few minutes to several hours or even longer.

Aggressive Behavior

Intense anger and a quick temper are common problems for individuals who have this mental disorder. It is difficult for them to maintain control over their emotions after they have been aroused due to this. They may rapidly become filled with fury, but this rage is not necessarily directed destructively, and it can end in self-harm. Sometimes a person's anger is directed only at oneself, rather than towards anybody or anything else.

Self-Harm

It is a potentially dangerous activity that may help a person feel better in a time of suffering. Many individuals suffering from BPD engage in self-harming behaviors, have suicidal thoughts, and make suicidal gestures and threats regularly. Many individuals with borderline personality disorder engage in sensation-seeking behavior that may be hazardous, particularly when agitated or depressed. Engagement in risky and unhealthy binge drinking, cutting or other self-injury, shopping and spending sprees, participating in hazardous sex regularly, and using drugs are examples of risky or intentional self-harm behaviors.

Not all instances of this act are meant to result in death. It's essential to note that it's often utilized to make people feel better when they're in a bad mood. But if left unchecked, these hazardous behaviors may lead to suicidal ideation and action.

Feelings of emptiness or worthlessness

A large number of individuals who suffer from the disease have feelings of emptiness or worthlessness. Many people who suffer from this problem describe feeling as if they have a vacuum inside them or don't matter. Consequently, people often resort to sex, drugs or food to attempt to feel fulfilled.

Feeling as though you are disconnected from reality.

Many people who have been diagnosed with this disorder have a skeptical attitude about occurrences in their life. It is difficult for them to cope with emotions of distrust and paranoia regarding the motives of others around them. While anxious, individuals may lose contact with reality and become disassociated from their surroundings. Being disassociated feels similar to being spaced out, hazy, or as if one exists outside of one's own body. Because it may be mistaken with other types of mental illness, getting a proper diagnosis is critical. Suppose you or someone close to you is experiencing frequent feelings of emptiness, loneliness, or insecurity that are causing irrationality or impulsivity. In that case, you must speak with your healthcare practitioner.

1.8 Treatment options for Borderline Personality Disorder

Psychotherapy is the primary treatment for this personality disorder, but medication may be used in conjunction with it. If your health is in danger, your doctor may suggest that you be admitted to the hospital. Treatment may assist you in developing the skills necessary to manage and deal with your illness. Other mental health problems, such as depression or drug abuse, that often co-occur with this personality disorder must also be addressed. With therapy, you may improve your self-esteem and lead a more secure and fulfilling life.

Psychotherapy

When treating this disorder, psychotherapy, often known as talk therapy, is a key therapeutic strategy. Your therapist may modify the kind of treatment you get to suit your specific requirements. The objectives of psychotherapy are to assist you in the following areas:

- Learn how to manage uncomfortable emotions.

- Reduce your impulsiveness by encouraging you to observe rather than act on them.

- Maintain a positive attitude toward your current ability to function.

- Improve your relationships by being aware of your own and others' feelings

- Educate yourself about borderline personality disorder.

Dialectical behavior therapy

It is a kind of treatment that involves both group and individual sessions that are especially intended to address borderline personality disorder. A skills-based approach teaches you to regulate your emotions better, cope with discomfort, and enhance your interpersonal interactions.

Schema-focused treatment

It is a kind of cognitive-behavioral therapy. Individual or group therapy may be utilized in conjunction with this treatment. It may assist you in identifying unmet needs that have resulted in negative life patterns that, although they may have been necessary for survival at one point, are now detrimental to your well-being in various areas. Therapy is concerned with assisting you in healthily meeting your needs to create good life patterns.

Cognitive-behavioral treatment

It is a kind of talk therapy that helps you recognize your thoughts and emotions at each given time and develop a new perspective on the issue. It is also known as behavioral therapy. It stresses the need to think before acting.

Systems training to improve emotional predictability and problem-solving abilities.

It is a twenty-week therapy that includes working in groups that include family members, carers, companions, and significant others participating in the program. It is a kind of psychotherapy that is used in conjunction with other types of treatment.

Transference focused therapy

Psychotherapy is centered on transference. It is also referred to as psychodynamic psychotherapy. The goal of this therapy is to assist you in understanding your emotions and interpersonal problems via the development of a therapeutic connection between you and your counselor. You next apply your newfound knowledge to current circumstances.

Adequate psychiatric supervision.

This therapy method is based on case management, with treatment expectations anchored in the expectation of involvement in a job or education. Rather than focusing on making sense of emotionally challenging times, it considers the interpersonal environment in which such emotions occur. It may include medication, group treatment, family education, and individual therapy, among other things.

Medications

Although there are currently no approved medicines for treating borderline personality disorder, some medications may effectively treat symptoms or co-occurring issues such as sadness, impulsiveness, aggressiveness, or anxiety associated with the condition.

- Antidepressants
- Antipsychotics
- Mood-stabilizing medications

Consult your doctor about the advantages and disadvantages of certain medicines.

Hospitalization

You may need more intensive therapy in a mental hospital or clinic at certain points in your life. Hospitalization may also be necessary to keep you safe from self-injury or to address suicidal thoughts or actions. Managing your emotions, thoughts, and actions takes time. Learning to control these things takes time as well. The majority of individuals recover significantly, but you may continue to battle with certain symptoms of borderline personality disorder for the rest of your life. Your symptoms may improve or worsen at different periods.

On the other hand, treatment may help you enhance your capacity to function and feel better about yourself. When you speak with a mental health professional who has expertise in treating borderline personality disorder, you have the greatest chance of achieving your goals.

02

Causes of Borderline Personality Disorder

For those who have this kind of personality disorder, you may be wondering what caused it or if you are to blame. The development of this illness is complicated, and there are likely several borderline personality disorder reasons to consider. However, it would help if you were certain that no single person or object is to blame for the development of it.

It is important to bear in mind the fact that the precise causes of this disorder are still not understood. For the time being, there are ideas that have some backing in the scientific community but are far from being definitive. To understand how and why the variables mentioned below are associated with it, further study is required.

Problem with the chemicals in the brain.

According to current research, the neurotransmitters in their brains, especially serotonin, malfunction in many personality disorder patients. Brain cells communicate via neurotransmitters, which are messenger chemicals produced by the brain. Reduced levels of the neurotransmitter serotonin have been associated with sadness, aggressiveness, and challenges in regulating harmful impulses.

An issue with brain growth.

Researchers have utilized magnetic resonance imaging to examine the brains of individuals who have this personality disorder. MRI scans, which utilize powerful magnetic fields and radio waves to create a precise picture of the body's interior, are becoming more popular. According to the findings, the scans showed that three brain areas were either smaller than anticipated or had very high activity levels in many individuals with it.

These were the sections:

- The amygdala – which has a key role in regulating emotions, particularly those considered "negative," such as anxiety, aggressiveness, stress.

- The hippocampus – which is involved in the regulation of behavior and self-control.

- An important part of the orbitofrontal cortex is engaged in planning and decision-making.

Your early life experiences and circumstances influence the development of these areas of the brain. According to some research, these brain areas are also important for mood regulation, which may explain some of the difficulties individuals with borderline personality disorder experience in intimate relationships.

Environmental Influences

According to a growing body of research, distressing childhood events, especially those involving caregivers, are strongly linked to BPD.

There are many different kinds of events that may be linked with it.

- Abuse that is physical or sexual.

- Neglect on an emotional or bodily level.

- Insensitivity on the part of the parents.

- Separation from primary caregivers at a young age.

- Exposition to long-term dread or discomfort as a kid.

• Suffering from parental neglect, whether by one or both parents
• The experience of growing up with a family member who suffered from a severe mental health illness, such as a personality disorder or a drinking or drug abuse problem.

The connection that a person has with their parents and family has a significant impact on how they view the world and what they think about other people in general.

Adult thought patterns skewed due to unresolved fear, wrath, and grief from childhood include those described below:
• Putting people in a positive light.
• Expecting others to act in the role of parent to you.
• Expecting other individuals to bully you.
• Acting as though other people are grownups when you are not one yourself.

These traumatic events may be concealed, and in some cases, disguised as praise.

2.1 Genetic Factors

While early research revealed that BPD is more likely to run in families, it remained unclear if this was due to environmental factors or genetics for a long time after that. There is currently some evidence that genetic factors and the environment play a major role in the development of autism. According to research, a mutation in the gene that regulates the way the brain utilizes serotonin, a naturally occurring neurotransmitter in the brain, is associated with this disorder.

According to the research, individuals with this particular variant of the serotonin gene may be more prone to develop it if they have previously had traumatic childhood experiences, for example, separation from supportive caregivers. Several studies have shown that monkeys with this gene variant exhibit symptoms comparable to this disorder, but only when separated from their mothers and reared in less loving settings. Monkeys with the gene variant that loving moms reared were much less likely to develop like symptoms than other monkeys with the gene variation.

You may be interested in learning more about the hereditary origins of this personality disorder. You are not alone in your feelings. Many individuals are perplexed as to why they, or a loved one, has this disorder. Unfortunately, there are no simple solutions, although research is progressing toward a better understanding of the origins of borderline personality disorder.

The findings of studies on it in families indicate that first-degree relatives of individuals treated for it are ten times more likely to have been treated for it themselves than relatives of those treated for schizophrenia or borderline illness, according to the findings. However, although this indicates that a personality disorder is passed down through families, research of this kind does not reveal how much of it is caused by genetics. This is because relatives share genes and share their surroundings in the majority of cases. For example, siblings may be raised by the same parents in the same household. As a result, these investigations may also reflect, to some extent, any environmental factors of this disorder.

Research

Studies have shown that genetics has a significant role in this personality disorder. A more direct, though still imprecise, method of investigating the impact of genes on it is to compare. It's the incidence of identical twins with fraternal twins in a family. Identical twins have the same genetic composition, while fraternal twins have genetic makeup similar to each other, much like two normal siblings. According to a few studies, 40 percent of its variance is driven by genetics, and the remaining 60 percent is caused by other variables, such as the environment, according to the researchers.

This indicates that personality disorder is a condition that is closely linked to hereditary factors. Nonetheless, it is most likely caused by a combination of genes and environment in most individuals who suffer from the condition.

What does this imply for you and your family?

If you suffer from this disorder, this implies that you are not to blame. You are most likely predisposed to developing the disease due to your genetic makeup. Perhaps you have also gone through some of the life experiences that have been associated with it in certain instances, such as being molested as a kid or losing a loved one, among other things. You do not have this because you are weak or unable to deal with life's difficulties. There is a reason why you are experiencing this symptoms.

If you have a close relative with this personality disorder, you may be more likely to get the condition yourself. However, there is no certainty that you will develop this disorder as a result of this. In reality, the odds are that you will not do so are high.

Why is treatment necessary?

If you are worried that you may be exhibiting symptoms of borderline personality disorder, you must get treatment as soon as possible. The risk factors will be reduced as a result, and your symptoms will be alleviated. Ask information to your doctor regarding your symptoms, any tests required for a thorough diagnosis, and any treatment choices.

2.2 Biological Factors

Multiple studies have shown that individuals with this personality disorder have abnormalities in their brain's structure and function in regions that regulate the feeling and expression of emotion. For example, individuals with this personality disorder exhibit higher activity levels in the limbic system, a part of the brain that regulates emotions such as fear, violence, and aggressiveness, than those who do not have a borderline disorder. Its signs of emotional instability may be associated with this. Newer research is also uncovering links between the hormone oxytocin and the development of borderline personality disorder.

2.3 Facts about Borderline Personality Disorder

It is common for the general public and even some healthcare professionals to misunderstand this personality disorder, a serious mental illness that affects the majority of the population, with the result of numerous misconceptions about this disorder. If you or someone you know suffers from it, it is critical to understand the illness's true nature to begin recovery. Here, we'll look at some facts that dispel common misconceptions about this disorder.

Borderline Personality Disorder can be managed.

Contrary to popular belief, this disorder can be treated. If you believe you have a borderline personality disorder, don't let this misconception keep you from seeking treatment or make you feel helpless. Being diagnosed with it does not imply that you will continue to experience the symptoms indefinitely. Hard work and effective treatment, such as psychotherapy, can significantly reduce the severity of its symptoms and may even allow you to lead a more normal life. If left untreated, these personality disorder symptoms will ebb and flow over time; some people can function higher than others so that recovery will look different for each individual.

Not all people who have this disorder are victims of childhood abuse.

Too often, well-intentioned individuals unfamiliar with such a personality disorder believe that it is caused by childhood abuse. This misunderstanding can have an impact on how they interact with people who have it. While some persons have been subjected to abuse, this is not the case for all individuals.

Children and adolescents may be diagnosed with it.

A borderline personality disorder is a psychic illness that may affect children and teenagers. However, identifying children or teenagers has proven contentious due to the widely held notion that a person's personality develops into adolescence. Officials have established precise criteria for diagnosing this personality disorder.

When making a diagnosis of any kind, caution should be used. This is particularly important since the symptoms may frequently be mistaken for those of normal teenage behavior. It may be necessary to seek a licensed professional therapist's expertise to differentiate between the two. Early diagnosis may be beneficial in ensuring that a person receives the treatment and support they need to begin their recovery.

Bipolar disorder and Borderline Personality disorder are two distinct disorders.

These disorders are two distinct conditions. Even though bipolar disorder and borderline personality disorder symptoms are relatively similar, they are two completely different diseases. Because healthcare professionals usually underestimate bipolar illness, individuals suffering from borderline personality are often misdiagnosed with bipolar disorder, thus compounding the misunderstanding.

It is also crucial to note that medicines used to treat bipolar illness often do not work for individuals with borderline personality disorder, making it necessary to see a therapist who has experience with it to get an accurate diagnosis and treatment plan.

Women are not the only ones who suffer from BPD.

While there was a school of thought that women were more often than males to be diagnosed with it, more recent research has shown similar percentages. However, how someone manifests symptoms of it may vary. While women are more likely to experience mood swings and feelings of emptiness, males are more likely to engage in impulsive conduct.

Everyone has different symptoms.

If you know one person suffering from a personality disorder, you don't know them all. Every individual is unique, and having this disorder does not alter this fact. To get its diagnosis, specific criteria must be fulfilled to the DSM-5, the gold standard in mental health treatment. Impairment in personality functioning as well as in interpersonal interactions is a criterion for eligibility. In each person, how these impairments manifest themselves is unique.

Furthermore, not all individuals who suffer from this disorder experience the same symptoms in the same manner. Your trouble in relationships may be different from someone else's problem in relationships. It manifests itself in a variety of ways for each individual.

2.4 The Relationship between Child Abuse and Borderline Personality Disorder

In reality, we don't yet know what causes this disorder, but it is thought to be a combination of biological and environmental variables. Evidence suggests that individuals with this personality disorder are more likely to disclose a history of child abuse or other traumatic childhood events. Despite this, many individuals who have suffered child abuse do not have it, and many people who have it were not mistreated or maltreated when they were children.

What is Child Abuse?

The word encompasses a broad variety of psychological and physical damage inflicted on a kid regarding child abuse.

Experts often assign this category to a collection of experiences such as:
• Being subjected to emotional assaults such as verbal abuse or degrading remarks.
• Abuse via bodily means, such as bruises or broken bones, is considered physical abuse.
• The act of being subjected to a sexual encounter or being exploited sexually by an adult is referred to as sexual abuse.

A significant proportion of individuals with this disorder have reported being abused as children throughout their childhood. People who have it say that they were sexually assaulted as children in a range of 45 to 75 percent of cases, and 20 percent to 70 percent indicate that they were physically abused as children.

As a result, although there has been a significant amount of research linking childhood abuse to it, there is also evidence that about one-third of individuals with this personality disorder do not report any abuse.

Other kinds of abuse may be more passive, such as physical neglect, in which a kid is denied basic needs such as food and water, for example. Emotional neglect is another kind of abuse in which a child's emotional needs are not met. No type of abuse is necessarily regarded as more severe than another; all forms of abuse may have long-term consequences for the victim and impact their psychological well-being. Both child abuse and neglect are associated with the development of psychiatric problems in children. The phrase child maltreatment is sometimes used to refer to children's physical abuse and psychological neglect.

Abuse of Children and Borderline Personality Disorder

According to recent research, evidence suggests that there is a link between child maltreatment and this personality disorder, according to recent research. Children and adolescents who suffer from it report high sexual abuse, emotional and physical abuse as children. This disease has also been linked to other types of child abuse, such as emotional and physical neglect. According to some studies, emotional and physical neglect may be more closely associated with its development than bodily or sexual abuse. This, however, is difficult to establish since children who are subjected to abuse are also often subjected to some neglect.

How may abuse contribute to BPD?

If childhood maltreatment is a risk factor for developing BPD, what are the mechanisms through which these early events contribute to the development of borderline personality disorder? According to the research findings, emotional abuse, in particular, may have a role in its development, and preoccupied adult attachment may mediate the abuse and the development of this disorder.

Other research has also looked at the effect of emotional abuse in developing this disorder and subsequent diagnosis. Even while these studies are essential in the search for reasons that may be avoided, they are also useful in identifying how therapy may assist individuals who are already dealing with the illness, particularly how methods involving emotion control may be particularly beneficial.

In addition to emotional exploitation, emotional invalidation has been linked to this personality disorder. However, it might be argued that being in such an environment is a kind of emotional abuse. When comparing its symptoms in individuals who were abused as children and those who were not, it has been shown that sexual abuse in childhood seems to be associated with a higher risk of suicidal ideation in persons with this disorder in particular.

What the Research has to say about it?

A link between this personality disorder and childhood abuse has been established pretty convincingly in research. There is no conclusive evidence that maltreatment is a contributing factor to it.A study that shows an association between two items does not always imply a causal relationship between the two things studied. Clearly, given the prevalence of child abuse data, which indicates that abuse is far more prevalent than expected, it is critical to establish whether or not abuse is a contributing factor to borderline personality disorder.

It is an illness that is often misunderstood. If you have a personality disorder or know someone who does, take the time to learn all you can about the condition. Contrary to common belief, it is curable, and people who suffer from it may have fulfilling lives. However, although its experience is often characterized by substantial difficulties in interpersonal interactions, this component of the illness may be significantly improved with knowledge from both the individual living with the disorder and those who care about them.

2.5 Emotional Invalidation and Borderline Personality Disorder

It may be caused by emotional invalidation experienced throughout childhood. The feeling of invalidation is common among individuals who have this personality disorder. Some experts think that invalidation may add to a child's likelihood of developing this disorder throughout adolescence or adulthood.

What is Emotional Invalidation and How does it happen?

When someone tells you that your feelings are not legitimate, illogical, or should be buried or altered, this is referred to as emotional invalidation. A parent may tell their kid to stop being such a baby when they feel frightened, saying, There's nothing to be afraid of. This reaction is emotionally invalidating' It not only conveys to the kid that their feelings are worthless but also implies that the child is weak for experiencing them. Alternatively, a parent could say something like, please tell me what makes you feel threatened. This is an example of a validating response. It communicates to the kid that their feelings are valued, even if the parent may not agree that there is an objective reason to be scared.

How it causes Borderline Personality Disorder?

This disorder is a mental illness that affects one's ability to regulate emotions. Many specialists think that emotional invalidation, especially throughout infancy and adolescence, adds to the development of this personality disorder. It has been suggested that an  emotionally nullifying environment, defined as an atmosphere in which one's emotional responses are consistently nullified or corrected, may interact with other factors to cause this personality disorder.

The model developed by Dr. Linehan proposes that infants at risk of developing it later in life are born with a biological tendency for powerful emotional reactions. Unfortunately, these strong emotional responses may be met with invalidation, which may, but does not necessarily, take the form of abuse or neglect. Note that this model connects the child's emotions and the surroundings, which is critical to understanding it. Because the child's emotional reactions to events that others may not respond to are so intense, their feelings are more likely to be dismissed as unimportant or unimportant. The likelihood of a parent or caregiver responding with behaviors that discourage the emotional response increases if the child's answers are seen as overreactions.

Discouragement of a kid's emotional reactions, especially if the youngster is temperamentally inclined to experience powerful emotions, is unlikely to be effective in calming the child. As a result, it is likely to have the opposite effect: the child's emotional reaction increases, resulting in an amplification of their feelings. More importantly, a kid who feels invalidated may lose out on the chance to learn how to successfully regulate her emotions, which may result in more emotional dysregulation down the line.

This model includes this invalidation as one risk factor, and there is fairly solid evidence of a link between childhood injustice and this personality disorder. Various forms of injustice, such as emotional neglect and physical abuse, inherently invalidate emotions. Researchers have shown that its signs are linked with reports of perceived early emotional invalidation. However, there is no way to know for certain if emotional invalidation is, in fact, a contributing factor to it.

Most of the research on this topic is retrospective, meaning that the researcher asks the person to report on experiences that occurred earlier in their life; these reports may be subject to bias and correlational, which means that it is based on a correlation between two variables meaning the analysis and results manifest a relationship between such emotional invalidation and this disorder but cannot conclude that invalidation is a cause of it.

2.6 Instructions on how to provide Emotional Validation

If you are reading this and in a relationship with someone who has BPD, you may have observed that some of your responses to their feelings have seemed to invalidate. Because a person with a personality disorder has such strong responses to little situations, it may not be easy to maintain a validating attitude toward them. Working with a mental health professional in person or online, on the other hand, may help you acquire techniques to enhance emotionally validating reactions and assist decrease your loved one's reactivity, whether in person or online.

A person's emotions are invalidated when the basis or validity of such feelings are attacked or called into doubt. This may be accomplished by rejecting, mocking, dismissing, or passing judgment on another's emotions or actions. The result is clear regarding how it is achieved: the person's emotions are wrong. When a kid grows up in an environment that he or she perceives as invalidating, he or she is likely to believe that his or her emotional reactions are not accurate or taken into account in the normal sequence of events. Over time, this may lead to confusion and a general mistrust of one's feelings on the part of the individual. Such an environment is not the same as an abusive one, even though abusive relationships are unquestionably invalidating in nature. Invalidation may be subtle, and it may be indicative of a general style of dealing with others. An intolerance usually characterizes this disorder to express emotional experiences, resulting in intense emotional outbursts.

Linehan, a personality disorder clinician and researcher, proposed the idea that the development of this disorder occurs during the developmental years when the child receives the message that he or she should learn to cope with emotions internally, without the support of his or her parents, and that this is when the child develops it. This results in the kid never learning how to control or endure her own emotions and failing to address the issues that are causing these emotions to be triggered.

Validation is not the same as recognition; rather, it is more of an acknowledgment of the individual, while appreciation is just a complimentary statement. To validate someone is to recognize the emotions expressed, regardless of whether you agree with what the other person believes. Appreciation focuses on the deed or conduct itself rather than on the emotion that motivated it. As a result, while a child's conduct is recognized and encouraged, the effort or bad feelings they are experiencing are not addressed in giving recognition. This may lead to the kid believing that his or her whole experience has been rejected, if not completely discarded.

A few examples may assist in illustrating how validation differs from praise and how invalidation can be changed as recognition in a much more understandable manner. On the first day of school, a little kid walks into the classroom by herself, although terrified. The simplest way to commend her would be to say, "Good work!" Alternatively, "You showed incredible bravery by going in even if you were terrified." Thy way you confirm the problematic emotions, acknowledges the work is required to overcome such thoughts and rewards the effort made to overcome those feelings. The following example shows how it is possible to praise while also invalidating: "Well. Don't you see how ridiculous you were acting before?" Even though the action was praised, this answer invalidates the emotions the kid was experiencing by referring to them as silly.

Those who have grown up with invalidating remarks, particularly those disguised as praise and encouragement, may find it difficult to distinguish between validating comments. The kid feels the pain that results from invalidation masked as praise, but others who are not directly engaged in the dynamics may be unaware of it. The effect of these invalidating remarks changed as the appreciation of a kid may not be recognized by other adults, who may discount the youngster's subsequent uneasiness or sorrow as a consequence of the child's over-sensitivity rather than a lack of forethought on the part of his or her parents.

It is essential to note that individuals tend to see relationships and interactions in a variety of different ways. This implies that what one person perceives as an invalidating environment is not necessarily seen in the same way by another person. Individual temperaments may influence a person's overall susceptibility to invalidation, although everyone experiences periods of vulnerability or sensitivity at various times during their lives.

The fact that invalidation is not a one-time event about borderline personality disorder development must be stressed. In most cases, this disorder is not caused by a single invalidating event but by a series of complicated and recurrent exposures to circumstances in which emotions and ideas are dismissed as irrelevant.

03

Types of Borderline Personality Disorder

According to Psych Central, the BPD is a mental illness that often manifests itself in adolescence or early adulthood and affects between 2 and 6 percent of the population in the US.

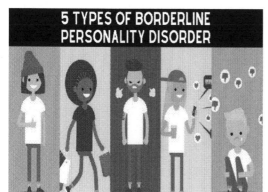

Because some of the symptoms may be mistaken for those of other illnesses, and because it often coexists with another condition, it is frequently misdiagnosed or overlooked entirely. The difficulty in establishing good relationships, severe mood fluctuations, and impulsivity, which may result in hazardous conduct, are the primary symptoms of a borderline personality disorder.

3.1 Common BPD Symptoms

If at least five of the following symptoms are present and form a chronic and repetitive pattern in a person, they are considered suffering from the disorder.

- Uncertainty about one's own identity.

- Thoughts of paranoia and dissociative nature.

- Periods of extreme rage that are not suitable.

- Feelings of emptiness or boredom that last for an extended time.

- A severe dread of being rejected and abandoned, whether real or imagined.

- Personal relationships are prone to swinging between idealization and devaluation.

- A state of emotional instability characterized by irritation and anxiety.

- Excessive impulsivity can result in reckless and harmful behavior.

People living with this personality disorder will go to any length to avoid any form of perceived abandonment or rejection, even if it means having extreme reactions to things like going on vacation or being a few minutes late to an appointment. These emotions can cause intense anger, which can then lead to impulsive and self-destructive behavior. Sometimes these actions are accompanied by suicidal inclinations, but the aim is not to carry out the plan fully.

Relationships are difficult for people with this disorder since emotions may rapidly change from deep affection to a sense that the receiver does not care enough or is not there for them. Most of the time, it creates disarray in all relationships, not just intimate ones, and it may even manifest itself in the job. Patients with this personality disorder are highly sensitive to their surroundings, and even apparently harmless occurrences may serve as triggers. It can damage oneself via impulsive ideas and behaviors, such as drug abuse, dangerous driving, eating disorders, body mutilation, uncertain sexual activity, and excessive spending.

According to studies, individuals diagnosed with this personality disorder are twice as likely as the general population to suffer from a drug addiction problem, most often associated with alcohol consumption. It is also characterized by an unstable sense of one's own identity or one's self-image. This may result in drastic shifts in one's objectives, profession, and other aspects of one's life. Opinions about oneself tend to swing from high to poor in a short time. People with this disorder have reported having unusual experiences and sensations of being separated from others.

3.2 Types of Borderline Personality Disorder

The several forms of this personality disorder, according to specialists, include the following:
• Quiet BPD
• Discouraged BPD
• Self-destructive BPD
• Impulsive BPD
• Petulant BPD

Some people who suffer from this disorder will fall into one of these subcategories, while others may fall into more than one category, depending on their circumstances. These symptoms may evolve and show themselves in a variety of ways throughout time. The discouraged BPD displays are clinging and codependent behavior, preferring to follow along in a group situation even though they feel down on their luck. They are typically overflowing with disappointment and fury under the surface, aiming towards others in their immediate vicinity. Such individuals who feel discouraged are more prone to indulge in self-mutilation and possibly suicide. They are looking for acceptance, but they also tend to avoid others, feel unworthy, and risk developing depression.

An impulsive personality is typically very charming, dynamic, and engaging in interactions with others. They may be shallow, flirty, and elusive, looking for thrills but getting soon bored with the situation. They live on attention and excitement, and they often get up in problems because they act first and think afterward, rather than the other way around. As a result, they may resort to drug addiction and self-injurious conduct to get acceptance from people around them and escape disappointment and rejection, respectively.

The petulant BPD is characterized by unpredictable behavior, irritation, stubbornness, and impatience. They tend to be obstinate, gloomy, and resentful, among other things. They balance on the precipice of severe emotions of unworthiness and wrath. They have the potential to erupt during these moments of rage. They are afraid of being let down by others, yet they can't seem to stop themselves from wanting to depend on them. They tend to be passive-aggressive and may engage in self-harming conduct to attract attention.

An individual who is on the self-destructive borderline participates in self-destructive conduct. They may or may not be conscious that they are engaging in harmful behavior at times. They are resentful and despise themselves. They have no concept of who they are and are frightened of being abandoned by their families. They may inflict physical harm on themselves in an attempt to feel anything. Those on the verge of self-destruction are more prone to indulge in hazardous conduct such as reckless driving and humiliating sexual activities.

Education is essential in treating any personality disorder. The more information you have, the easier it will be to deal with the problem. Identifying a subtype or discovering that you do not fit into a particular one may aid in the understanding and treatment of this disorder.

3.3 Quiet Borderline Personality Disorder

Although you may be acquainted with such a personality disorder, this disease has many subtypes. It has many subtypes, one of them is a quiet borderline personality disorder, which implies that you focus your problems more inside so that others do not notice. It isn't easy to identify and treat it; nevertheless, the sooner you get treatment, the better the result. Here's everything you need to know about the situation.

What exactly is quiet BPD?

It is possible to have a silent personality disorder, which implies that you focus any mood swings and actions inside rather than outward toward others. For lack of a better phrase, you act in rather than act out. Acting inward may exacerbate a mental disorder that is already difficult to detect. It is characterized by focusing important emotions onto oneself while not allowing other people to perceive them.

The following are examples of strong emotions:
• Anger
• Anxiety

• Rage
• Extreme self-doubt
• Attachments/obsessions based on emotions.
• Apprehension of being abandoned or rejected.
• Mood swings are a common occurrence.
• Self-blame and guilt are two emotions that people experience.

It is sometimes referred to as high-functioning borderline personality disorder in certain circles. The use of this phrase may be deceptive since it implies that a person suffering from this kind of disorder does not necessarily display their symptoms and is nonetheless capable of coping in daily settings such as work and school.

What are the signs and symptoms of quiet BPD?

Because an inner focus characterizes this type of disorder, it may be difficult to distinguish from other forms of borderline personality at first.

The following are some of the most noticeable symptoms of silent borderline personality disorder:
• A person with very low self-esteem.
• Emotions such as numbness or emptiness.
• Suicidal ideation or self-harming behavior.

- Emotions of guilt and humiliation are constant.

- A deep-seated dread of being rejected.

- Anxiety in social situations and self-isolation.

- Possessing thin skin and taking criticism personally.

- Feeling as though you are a burden to everyone around you.

- Feeling disconnected from the outside world and occasionally having the sensation of being in a dream.

- People-pleasing, even at the expense of one's well-being.

- Being afraid of being alone but yet pushing others away at the same time.

- Difficulty in establishing relationships with other people.

- The ability to experience mood fluctuations may last as short as a few hours or as long as a few days while no one else can see them.

- Suppression of emotions of rage or denial of the fact that you are furious. When you're angry, you should retreat.

- Avoiding conversing with people who have offended you and shutting them off as a result

> - When there is a disagreement, you place the blame on yourself.

It would be best if you kept in mind that some individuals with this condition may only have a few of these symptoms, while others may experience all or a combination thereof.

Negative effects of Quiet BPD

Many individuals suffering from this condition suffer in silence for fear of becoming a burden to others. However, if left untreated, the symptoms may deteriorate with time. An increased chance of developing additional mental illnesses.

This kind of borderline illness may raise your chance of developing other mental health problems, such as:

- Anxiety illnesses
- Bipolar disorder
- Depression
- Eating disorders
- Anxiety in social situations
- Substance abuse

It isn't easy to develop and maintain connections. With this type of BPD, it may be difficult to form and maintain relationships, and some of the associated symptoms can make things more challenging in this regard. You may find it difficult to connect emotionally with people due to the continuous war between fear of being hurt and fear of being alone that you experience. Maintaining a regular job or school routine is difficult. It may also become more difficult for you to retain your position at work or school as time passes.

In the absence of treatment, you may be more likely to behave impulsively and engage in risky behaviors such as excessive spending, gambling, and drinking, among other things. Self-harm and suicide ideation are possible outcomes. Suicidal thoughts and acts, as well as self-harm, are possible outcomes.

Suicidal feelings or words should always be treated with extreme caution.
• Keep an eye on the individual until assistance comes.
• Remove any weapons, knives, medicines, or other items that may be used to hurt someone.
• Listen without interjecting with judgment, argument, threat, or yelling.

How is Quiet BPD caused?

It is not an exception to the rule that mental disorders are frequently inherited. According to one research, personality problems throughout infancy were associated with substantial hereditary influences. Adults suffering from it are more likely to have a family history of the disorder. Genetics are not the sole factor contributing to the development of this disorder in children and adolescents. The researchers have also observed that emotional and physical abuse and early neglect may raise an individual's chance of developing schizophrenia.

It is also possible that exposure to unstable relationships or personal history has a role. Changes in the neurotransmitter serotonin have been linked to this disorder. However, it is unclear whether brain alterations cause it or arise as a result of the disorder.

Who is at risk for developing Quiet BPD?

Several risk variables have also been identified as having an impact on the development of this condition.

A history of the following may be included:
• Substance addiction
• Eating disorders
• Anxiety or sadness
• Abandonment or neglect.

What is the procedure for diagnosing Quiet BPD?

It is often mistaken as another illness, such as depression or social anxiety, due to common misunderstandings and the inner character of the condition. Even though various symptoms may coexist, it is a distinct diagnosis that a mental health expert can only make. After interviewing with you, a licensed mental health practitioner may make its diagnoses, such as a psychiatrist or psychologist.

Additionally, they may ask you to participate in a survey based on your symptoms to get more information. Even while there is no medical test for quiet borderline personality disorder, having your symptoms checked by a doctor may help rule out other illnesses causing your symptoms. Important to disclose to your healthcare practitioner is any personal or family history of personality disorder or other common co-occurring illnesses such as anxiety, depression, mental ailment, or eating disorders.

An online survey for borderline personality disorder that you may complete at your leisure may also be beneficial in guiding you toward a diagnosis. Keep in mind that such online tests should not be used instead of an in-person consultation with a mental health expert. It may be difficult to diagnose oneself with a mental disorder.

What is the treatment for Quiet Borderline Personality Disorder?

Even though it may be tough to acknowledge the need to speak with someone about your problems, doing so will probably provide you with a feeling of freedom and affirmation. When treating it, psychodynamic therapy, dialectical behavior therapy, and psychiatric medicines are the first lines of defense.

Dialectical behavior therapy emphasizes on :
• Mindfulness methods
• Emotional regulation
• Distress tolerance
• Interpersonal effectiveness,

With time and repetition, this may assist in reducing self-destructive ideas and behaviors. A psychotherapist administers this therapy. If prescribed by a psychiatrist, certain mental health medicines may effectively alleviate some of your symptoms. However, it would be best not to depend only on medicines to treat your disorder since they may not often address the underlying reasons for the disorder. Such medicines are often most effective when used in combination with psychotherapy.

The signs of this disorder may be difficult to recognize, but the sooner you recognize them, the sooner you can begin to take action. It's important to understand that your emotions are valid and that it's completely okay to express them to other people. While you may be struggling in the background with constant guilt and low self-esteem, the reality is that you deserve to have a happy and full life.

3.4 Discouraged Borderline Personality Disorder

Suppose you have understood all the borderline personality disorders via personal experience with a person who suffers from the condition or through your battle with the disorder. In that case, the path has most likely been a difficult one for you to navigate. For individuals who have this personality disorder, life is like riding a rollercoaster while wearing a blindfold. Not

only are the highs and lows intense and often back-to-back, but they are also unexpected and unpredictable.

This disorder is characterized by impulsivity and instability, two of the most prominent characteristics of the disorder, which Adolph Stern first described. Many people with this condition have low self-respect, the anxiety of abandonment, and anger problems. When someone suffers from it, they become very sensitive to criticism or any other kind of perceived rejection. Those suffering from this condition tend to view most elements of life as either black or white.

Their extreme way of thinking results in a with or against me attitude to evaluate relationships at all complexity levels. People involved in a sufferer's life are often romanticized and seen as unusually wonderful, or they are demeaned and perceived as exceptionally terrible, if not downright evil.

According to the psychologist, people suffering from the condition were previously characterized as having no emotional skin.

How does Discouraged BPD affect you?

When a person has this personality disorder, the dependent elements of their personality disorder drive a large portion of their thoughts, feelings, and behaviors. In fact, according to studies, from the outside, a person with this disorder may seem to be similar in appearance to someone with a dependent personality. This individual exhibits symptoms of codependence in the majority of his or her relationships throughout life.

It is frequently most apparent when a discouraged borderline type personality becomes reliant on someone dependency is not acceptable. For example, a casual relationship or a companion or lover with whom they have just recently begun dating, that they have grown dependent on them. It is possible for someone suffering from this kind of borderline disorder to seem sad or serious on the outside, particularly when contrasted to the other personality disorder subtypes.

It is easy to identify this type of disorder because of their obvious clinginess and passive follower attitude. While on the surface, this person may seem doubtful or, at worst, weak-willed, on the inside, they are usually filled with anxiety and resentment toward people around them because of their lack of leadership and ability to motivate others. If someone has this kind of personality disorder, they may resort to self-harming behaviors such as self-mutilation or suicide.

Who is most affected by Discouraged BPD?

Borderline personality disorder and its discouraged borderline variant may affect men and women of any ethnicity or socioeconomic background, but the diagnosis is more common in women than males. This may be linked to a potential neurobiological issue like as low estrogen levels, or it could be due to a prejudice generated by traditional sexism, among other things. According to some studies, women are more likely than males to seek therapy, be urged to seek treatment, and be formally diagnosed or misdiagnosed with the illness. It affects both men and women, according to other research. This diagnosis is generally made throughout adolescence, at the earliest, and it is typically made before the end of adolescence or the beginning of early adulthood.

Signs and Symptoms of Discouraged BPD

According to the DSM-V, there are many indications and symptoms of this type of personality disorder.

These are regarded to be defects in the functioning of the personality and impairments in one's ability to function. Such deficits may include:

- Having an unstable or bad self-image.

- Engaging in excessive self-criticism.

- Experiencing persistent sensations of emptiness.

- Experiencing stress-induced dissociative episodes.

- Deteriorations in interpersonal communication and interaction.

- Additionally, objectives, beliefs, job plans, and general aspirations may be subject to change or instability.

Such impairments might include low levels of empathy, which can manifest as a reduced ability to understand the perspectives of others, high and dramatic sensitivity to perceived criticism or rejection, the vast majority of people are viewed as either good or bad. Aspects of interpersonal functioning that are impaired may include problems with intimacy, for example. These problems may manifest themselves as very intense and unstable relationships characterized by great disagreement, doubt, clinginess, a fear of abandonment, and either over-involvement or withdrawal at various points in the relationship's development.

Additionally, there are additional indicators that a person has borderline personality as opposed to others. Some of these signs and symptoms may include the following:

- Moodiness

- Shame

- Impulsivity

- Dread of being rejected.

- Emotions that are easily aroused.

- Emotional sensations that are unstable.

- Uncertainty causes a sense of unease.

- Dread of losing one's grip on things.

- The stress-induced sense of urgency.

- Suicidal thoughts or actions are not uncommon.

- Feelings of discouragement or hopelessness

- Having difficulty coming up with or adhering to plans.

- Anxiety which is associated with separation.

- Affective responses that are considerably more strong or disproportionate to their underlying cause.

- Nervousness, pressure, concern, panic, or generalized anxiety are all symptoms of increased stress.

- Fixation on painful memories from the past or the possibility of unpleasant memories in the future Fear and uncertainty are common emotions.

- Extreme dependence, loss of autonomy, or the dread of an inevitable loss of one's identity are all attachment disorder symptoms.

- Dangerous risk-taking conduct that is not concerned with the repercussions

- Anger, particularly when it is directed towards or in response to recognized judgment or rejection

- Disassociation, often known as zoning out and trouble focusing, are common.

The following are some borderline personality disorder symptoms that are unique to the discouraged borderline disorder:

- Abuse of drugs and alcohol.

- Loyalty, even to the point of becoming extreme.

- Feelings of insecurity and helplessness.

- Dependence on others to an excessive degree.

- Episodes that brought tears to my eyes

- Emptiness and a sense of desolation.

- Constant emotions of being on the verge of losing one's life.

- Feeling hopeless, incapable, powerless, and sad is a common experience.

- One is pliant and readily persuaded when it comes to others, even when it goes against one's wishes.

- Even while seeking a starring position, she remains submissive and meek.

- As a consequence of poor self-esteem, uncertainty, and vulnerability, one feels humble.

- The act of persecuting and victimizing oneself; the belief that others are continuously assaulting or ill-intentioned.

- Whether via physical aggression against objects or through a cycle of collecting and then giving away or selling objects, destruction or deliberate loss of possessions are both prohibited.

- Reliance on imagination as a method of escape, typically shown via participation in fantasy-based media (novels, films, comics, etc.)

- Symptoms of chronic or recurrent disease, including somatic complaints

- Deprivation of one's own needs which is based on emotions of worthlessness

Causes and Negative Effects

In the same way that many mental health illnesses are difficult to diagnose, pinpointing the exact etiology of this disorder or its discouraged subtype is challenging. Researchers believe that the underlying etiology of this disease is complex and not readily or immediately recognized by the general public. Many experts in the area appear to agree on several possible contributing reasons for this personality disorder, even though the disorder is considered diverse and complicated, including many distinct life circumstances.

Some of these factors and their relationships are as follows:

- It may be associated with post-traumatic stress disorder.

- Factors related to the nervous system, such as estrogen levels

- Aside from trauma, environmental variables such as family and societal stability also have a role.

- Social variables, such as social experiences as a kid, are important.

- Childhood trauma, especially abuse and neglect, which often includes sexual abuse, is a serious problem.

- Congenital brain abnormalities, such as a smaller hippocampus or amygdala, may be present at birth.

- In genetics, specifically in the genes DRD4 and DAT, as well as on chromosome nine.

Diagnosis of Discouraged BPD

Diagnosing this disorder and its subcategories is not always straightforward, even for the most experienced mental health professionals. According to a scientific study, the diagnosis of this type of illness is often incorrect in some way or another. An additional complication is that women with the condition are especially susceptible to developing co-occurring disorders, making a correct diagnosis even more difficult. Major depression, stress disorders, eating troubles, drug dependence, and antisocial personality are among the diseases that are often reported to be comorbid with a borderline personality disorder. Many of these co-occurring illnesses are characterized by poor self-esteem or an unstable sense of self.

Treatment of Discouraged BPD

Patients with this personality disorder need effective management and therapy to live productive and happy lives to the best of their ability. This is particularly essential since this mental disorder entails a significant risk of suicide. People who have it account for a significant proportion of all suicide attempts each year; thus, any self-harm or suicidal inclinations on a person who has it should be handled promptly and treated extremely seriously. You or someone you know must get assistance as soon as possible if you or they are contemplating suicide.

Psychotherapy is the most common technique for managing and treating this type of personality disorder. However, although no one drug can treat all of the symptoms of this disorder, several of the comorbid illnesses that often accompany the disorder may be addressed with prescription medication, improving the overall success rate of therapy. Understanding that these medicines cannot cure this disorder is critical but understanding that the treatment of concurrent illnesses may pave the path for more effective treatment via psychotherapy is also critical.

Depression and anxiety are two of the most frequent comorbid disorders treated with medication while the patient is being treated for a general personality disorder with psychotherapy. When taken in conjunction with other medicines, antipsychotics may help decrease impulsive and suicidal thoughts and anxiety, sadness, and psychotic paranoia symptoms.

When treating a patient with a borderline personality disorder, it is critical to identify and treat any comorbid diseases in the patient's body. Before therapy can begin in earnest, it is necessary to address any comorbid conditions and start treatment. For example, drug addiction, often associated with it, needs to be eliminated as a contributing cause of the disordered behavior before real therapy can begin. Otherwise, a patient's cognitive function may be hindered, making it impossible for a professional to conduct an appropriate examination of the patient.

3.5 Self-Destructive Borderline Personality Disorder

Feeling of loneliness and humiliation, relationship problems, mood changes, and impulsive conduct are symptoms of such a borderline personality disorder, which may manifest in various ways. To better classify the symptoms of this disorder, Theodore developed four subtypes of this disorder that may be classified further. Many individuals with this disorder fall into one or two of these categories, and it is uncommon for them to be evenly divided between the characteristics of all four. Don't anticipate your symptoms to be a perfect match for anyone subtype; instead, look to see whether one or two categories reflect your behavior more accurately than the others. Your therapy will be more effective if you are knowledgeable about your condition.

How is it to have Self-Destructive BPD?

There was a boy named John. His father, who divorced his mother and went away when John was a toddler, left him to grow up without his mother's support. Although his mother suffered from chronic depression and other mental health issues, John managed to establish friends, achieve academic success, and compete on the football team at his high school. Even though no one knew it, he grew up despising himself to such an extreme degree that he could never imagine anybody else feeling the same way about him. He felt, in his heart of hearts, that he was unworthy of love and affection. John tended to sneak into his mother's liquor cupboard before she arrived home to dull the pain of saying the wrong thing in class, making a mistake at football practice, or feeling like an outcast among his peers.

John met Anna during his junior year of high school, and the two began dating. In her company, he had brief moments of respite from his severe self-hatred, interspersed with many more times of great dread that she would abandon him since how could she possibly love him as much as she claimed? Anna was a role model for him. He considered her to be the most important person in his life. In the spring of her senior year, Anna informed John that she had applied to a university outside of the state and had been admitted with a full scholarship. When John found out, he felt betrayed since they intended to attend the same local state institution. His feelings were too much for John to handle; he couldn't believe he had allowed himself to imagine Anna loved him, that she had ever cared about him, or that she may even stay around. He informed Anna that she would be unable to leave him; his suicide would be the result if she did.

After Anna returned home, he barricaded himself in his room with booze and a weapon and dialed Anna's phone to say his last farewell. John's closest buddy had to climb up the house to his second-story bedroom window to calm him down and keep him safe on that particular evening.

Symptoms of Self-Destructive BPD

John was diagnosed with a borderline personality disorder subtype that was self-destructive.

Before beginning therapy at the institute, he exhibited many of the characteristics of self-destructive personality disorder, including the following:
• Abuse of drugs and alcohol
• Suicidal ideation and behavior
• Angry and resentful feelings
• Uncertainty about one's own identity.
• Self-loathing emotions are very strong.
• Susceptible to self-harm and often sad.
• Seek consolation from others' attention to feel better.
• Self-destructive behavior is a kind of conduct that causes harm to oneself.

- Indulge in risky conduct due to a lack of self-care rather than to impress others.

- They have a tendency to undermine their pleasure and well-being because they believe they are unworthy.

- They believe that no one is concerned about them, and as a result, they do not care about themselves.

Behavioral Therapy for Self-Destructive BPD

Someone who leans toward this subtype is more likely to seek therapy than someone who does not. This is due to the deeply ingrained sentiments of poor self-worth that they have developed through time. Even though you have this subtype of a personality disorder, you are not an exception to the rule that this is a curable illness. In the months after John graduated from high school, he fought the notion of going to residential treatment for almost a year.

His feelings of profound guilt and self-hatred about how he had been feeling and about the fact that he had dragged people into his dark and twisted world came flooding back to him after the night he threatened to commit suicide to Anna. His mother set up an appointment for him to visit a therapist. He attended appointments, but he did not find therapy beneficial, and he often left sessions feeling even worse about himself. As the year progressed, suicide attempts and threats grew more frequent. His mother recognized the severity of his condition led her to persuade him to engage in residential treatment. As he stepped through the doors, he was filled with apprehension and a glimmer of optimism.

John was able to go through his father's desertion with the assistance of a private therapist, which assisted him in gradually healing that profoundly painful scar. John thought that the dialectical behavior therapy skills group and learning cognitive behavioral therapy in his sessions were the most beneficial of his treatment groups. He enjoyed that he didn't feel embarrassed about being the way he was while he worked at the institute. He wasn't the only one who felt this way. Instead, he felt encouraged by his fellow participants, and he became more hopeful as he saw the improvement made by other borderline patients.

Working with his career and education counselors throughout the program, John discovered a new love for woodworking and decided to enroll in a carpentry trade school. As John progressed through the program, he discovered that he enjoyed working with them. He discovered beneficial hobbies that helped him divert his attention away from unpleasant feelings, decreasing his desire to participate in self-destructive behaviors and assisting him in his recovery from drug and alcohol addiction.

Upon leaving the institute, John had the knowledge and skills necessary to maintain good interpersonal connections, pursue a rewarding job and develop a strong sense of self that would enable him to withstand the challenges that life would throw at him. His greatest confidence came from knowing that he could withstand these assaults and get back up on his feet.

3.6 Impulsive Borderline Personality Disorder

An impulsive type of borderline personality disorder is one of the four kinds of personality disorders. This specific subtype of disorder is the most dramatic of the available options. According to a psychologist, the impulsive subtype has several characteristics with a histrionic personality disorder.

Signs and Symptoms of Impulsive BPD

A person who has this personality disorder is more likely to exhibit the signs and symptoms of the subtype listed below:

- Captivating and with a natural charm.

- Complaints of a chronic or recurrent medical condition.

- Adolescents who engage in attention-seeking practices.

- High amounts of energy and a tendency to get bored.

- Thrill-seeking and risk-taking behaviors that are not concerned with the repercussions.

- Manipulative and deceptive of others, especially while attempting to establish oneself as the focus of attention.

- Other people find you attractive, sometimes without even recognizing it.

- When you're superficial, you may easily amuse people on the surface level while avoiding deeper significant encounters or connections.

This subtype's signs and symptoms coincide with or complement some of other personality disorder's more common signs and symptoms.

Causes of Impulsive BPD

The field of mental disease is where pinpointing the precise etiology of a problem may be difficult to achieve success. This is because mental disorders are complicated and are currently undergoing many studies that will one day allow us to understand their causes better. At this point, mental disorders are considered to be the consequence of various causes, none of which we know to be more significant than the others in their effect.

These are a few of the reasons that may contribute to this disorder:
• Genetics
• Social issues
• Childhood trauma
• Brain abnormalities
• Environmental factors
• Psychological factors
• Neurobiological variables

Much research is still being conducted on personality disorders, the impulsive subtype, and the causes and connections between the two. We do know that the following problems have a role.

Trauma During Childhood

Its patients have a high prevalence of childhood trauma. Abuse and neglect are among the most frequent childhood traumas that have been recorded among those who have suffered from them, and sexual abuse is one of the most common types of abuse. Researchers have also discovered a significant prevalence of caregiver loss and incest in the childhoods of individuals who have this disorder. People who have it as adults often claim that their caretakers throughout their childhood frequently rejected the legitimacy of their emotions and failed to provide them with the safety they need as children. People with this disorder have exhibited emotionally distant and inconsistent conduct with their carers.

Factors Associated with Neurobiology

Having low levels of estrogen has been linked to borderline personality disorder in certain studies. These kinds of abnormal estrogen levels are sometimes seen in ladies throughout their menstrual cycle. However, severe PMS must be treated differently than personality disorder and that hormone-related therapy not be started on patients who also have endometriosis.

Abnormalities of the Brain

Various brain abnormalities have been identified in those who have this personality disorder. There is a reduction in the size of the amygdala and the hippocampus, for example. According to research, the prefrontal cortex is typically less active in individuals with personality disorders than in those who do not have the illness. Additionally, cortisol production is often increased in individuals who have it. There are many possible causes for this overproduction of cortisol, including traumatic childhood experiences, which may stimulate cortisol production or a preexisting high level of cortisol production that can lead patients to perceive events as traumatic.

Genetics

The heritability of this personality disorder is a major focus of causative study into the disorder. According to current estimates, it has a heritability factor of about 60 percent. According to the research findings, genetic influences account for 40 percent of the variance in its characteristics among patients, and borderline personality disorder traits are associated with chromosome nine. DRD4, which has also been linked with disordered attachment, and DAT, which has been associated with inhibitory control problems, are two more genes that are now being investigated for their potential involvement in the development of borderline personality disorder.

The Influence of Other Factors

Researchers are also investigating if any additional variables may be contributing to the development of this disorder. A stable family unit may help to prevent the development of this disease. As a result, certain variables such as family stability and social stability are being investigated to see whether they can play a role in the development of this disorder.

Diagnosis of Impulsive BPD

It has traditionally been a difficult condition to detect and diagnose correctly. Since Stern originally coined the term, mental health practitioners have battled to clarify the parameters of diagnosis and therapy for individuals who have this personality disorder. Various problems obscure the evaluation of borderline personality disorder in a clinical environment, all of which have contributed to the complexity of this kind of assessment.

There is a significant incidence of comorbidity among those who have this problem. Major depression, anxiety disturbances, drug dependence, antisocial personality dysfunction, and eating disorders are all common among individuals with this disorder, among other illnesses. The presence of these symptoms may make it harder for someone to detect this disorder from a distance, and some of these problems, such as drug addiction, can significantly impair a person's cognitive function and treatment outcomes.

Management of Impulsive BPD

The ups and downs of daily life may be overwhelming at times, but therapy can completely transform the way a person absorbs and manages their condition. A person who has this personality disorder must get treatment as soon as possible. Delaying treatment can worsen the disease, which may progress to the point of being extremely debilitating over time. Furthermore, this disorder is responsible for a significant number of suicides each year. As a result, any instances of self-harm or suicidal thoughts or actions of a person suffering from it must be addressed and treated immediately.

Psychotherapy

Psychotherapy has a significant role in the treatment of borderline personality disorder.

The following therapies are used to treat it:
• Cognitive-behavioral therapy
• Transference-focused psychotherapy
• Dialectical behavior therapy
• Mentalization-based treatment
• Schema-focused therapy
• General psychiatric management

•

Mentalization behavioral therapy and Dialectical behavioral therapy are two of the most effective treatment approaches, but the key to a successful recovery is figuring out what works best for each particular person.

Medication

Although no prescription drug can be used to treat this disorder, prescriptions are often used to assist control illnesses that occur to provide a more effective overall therapy. Medications may be used to treat anxiety, sadness, rage, and impulsivity, for example, while the fundamental problems of this personality disorder are addressed without the detrimental distraction of the other concerns. The medical care of these co-occurring problems is not only beneficial, but it is also often seen as essential in the treatment of this personality disorder.

It is critical to recognize that there is no known cure for it, but medication is available to treat the disease's symptoms. Treating the concurrent problems is just a question of paving the way for a more accurate and effective therapy in the future. Being a person with impulsive type disorder does not have to be a constant uphill battle. Even though the ups and downs of daily life may be overwhelming at times, therapy can significantly alter the way a person absorbs and manages their condition.

3.7 Petulant Borderline Personality Disorder

This borderline personality disorder is characterized by pessimism, resentment, critical thinking, indirect aggression, restlessness, and a tendency to be quickly disappointed. They may respond in a rebellious and obstinate manner to perceived slights if they do not think about it. In their relationships, people with this subtype are often unpredictable, frequently engage in a push-pull dynamic in which they feel a strong desire for others and then push them away. Individuals with paranoid disorders and depressive disorders are more likely to show the features of these illnesses.

Signs and Symptoms
• Extreme mood swings
• Anxious in social situations
• Passive-aggressive behavior
• A desire to exert control over others

- In relationships, there is a lot of push and pull.

- Others are being excluded from their life.

- Fear of being abandoned to an extreme degree.

- Using ultimatums in interpersonal interactions.

- A lack of capacity to communicate one's emotions.

- Suicidal inclinations are common among adolescents.

- Experiencing discontent in one's interpersonal connections

- Angry outbursts and feelings of unworthiness and unwanted are common.

- Co-occurring illnesses, such as drug addiction and eating disorders.

- Suspicion of others and paranoia in interpersonal interactions

- Proof that someone doesn't care about her Constantly looking for affirmation

- It is the desire for others to feel bad about their acts or lack of actions.

> - Using suicidal or self-injurious conduct to exert control over others is called coercion.

Treatment

Most petulant borderline personality disorder behaviors are motivated by a fear of abandonment, a sense of personal inadequacy, and an inability to calm oneself. Fortunately, with the proper therapy, you may conquer your personality disorder and go forward. Psychotherapy and different medications are used to treat it.

04

Diagnosis of Borderline Personality Disorder

When a person has a personality disorder, their relationships become unstable, experience severe mood swings, and have an unstable self-image. The disease may cause a great deal of discomfort and suffering, both for individuals who have it and those who care about them. An accurate diagnosis is often a

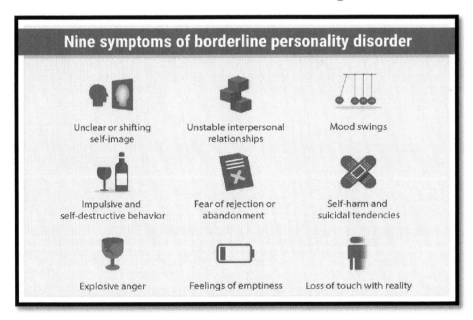

Nine symptoms of borderline personality disorder

Unclear or shifting self-image

Unstable interpersonal relationships

Mood swings

Impulsive and self-destructive behavior

Fear of rejection or abandonment

Self-harm and suicidal tendencies

Explosive anger

Feelings of emptiness

Loss of touch with reality

source of comfort; at long last, an explanation for years of perplexing behavior. Treatment is made possible via accurate diagnosis. Learn how healthcare professionals diagnose personality disorders and differentiate them from other mental illnesses.

4.1 How do we diagnose Borderline Personality Disorder?

People who exhibit symptoms of such a personality disorder, such as impulsive behavior, recklessness, an unstable self, significant mood changes, and background of relationship problems, should be evaluated by a mental health professional to determine whether they have the disorder. Clinical social workers and psychologists licensed to practice in their respective states can assess and treat mental health problems. Primary healthcare professionals, such as doctors and family physicians, are not qualified to diagnose this disorder; however, they can refer you to a mental health professional with the knowledge and experience you require.

Although there is no test for diagnosing a personality disorder, your doctor may ask you to complete mental health questionnaires or participate in psychological tests and assessments to learn more about your personality. The symptoms, life experience, and family history of the patient are all gathered by mental health professionals to make an accurate diagnosis. By giving your physician comprehensive information about your symptoms, you may aid him or her in arriving at an appropriate diagnosis. It will be important for your physician to know when your symptoms first appeared, which ones you experience the most frequently, and how they interfere with your personal and professional life. As part of the interview process, your physician will likely ask questions about your family and upbringing.

According to research, people who have a parent or sibling with personality disorders are more likely to have the condition themselves. Therefore, if someone in your family has a borderline disorder, the chances that you will as well are increased. Answer all of the questions about your family and childhood as honestly as possible, even if it is painful to do so. A history of shock, abuse, or negligence increases the likelihood of developing it in the future. In some cases, your provider may recommend that you undergo a complete medical examination by a physician to rule out any physical causes for your symptoms.

4.2 Diagnostic Criteria for Borderline Personality Disorder

According to the Diagnostic and Statistical Manual of Mental Disorders, you must show five out of the nine symptoms listed below to be diagnosed with any borderline personality disorder:

- Reckless driving

- Substance abuse

- Extremely erratic mood swings

- A persistent sense of emptiness

- Inappropriate sexual behavior

- A strong fear of being abandoned.

- Uncertainty about one's own identity

- Impulsive, potentially dangerous behavior

- Experiencing inappropriate or uncontrolled rage

- A pattern of instabilities in interpersonal relationships

- Self-harming behavior (such as cutting) or attempted suicide.

- Suspicious thoughts, delusions, or a temporary loss of contact with reality.

Many of these symptoms are also associated with other types of mental health problems. Schizophrenia is characterized by extreme mood fluctuations, which are a hallmark sign of borderline illness. Paranoia, on the other hand, is a typical symptom of schizophrenia.

On the other hand, paranoid episodes linked with personality disorder are usually short, while individuals with schizophrenia may suffer from paranoia that lasts for a lengthy period. Details like this assist healthcare professional in distinguishing between mental health disorders that have common characteristics. However, because borderline personality disorder is frequently found in conjunction with other mental

health conditions such as attention deficit or hyperactivity disorder, anxiety issues, post-traumatic stress disorder, personality disorder and depression, it can take a long time for mental health providers to sort through symptoms and behavior to make an accurate diagnosis of a personality disorder.

4.3 Why is Borderline Personality Disorder misdiagnosed?

It is sometimes identified after another condition, such as ADHD, has been diagnosed in the individual. As long as your symptoms continue after therapy for it, you and your physician will begin to consider the existence of another mental health disorder, such as borderline personality disorder. Inform your healthcare practitioner if you continue to have symptoms after receiving a diagnosis and treatment.

There are numerous reasons why living with a personality disorder is difficult, including dysfunctional families, negative emotionality and dysregulation, impulsive conduct, and other challenging characteristics. However, the condition is even more difficult to deal with because many people who suffer from it are completely unaware that they have it.

It is one of the most frequently misdiagnosed mental health conditions, accounting for approximately five percent of all cases. The condition is so commonly misdiagnosed that there isn't even an accurate prevalence rate available for the condition. However, we only have estimates of 2 to 6 percent of the population suffering from it, making it a very common condition. So, how is it possible that such a common condition can be misdiagnosed so frequently? Here are a few possible explanations for why this might be the case:

Social Stigma

One of the most stigmatized mental health disorders a person can suffer from is a personality disorder. This widespread stigma has measurable and social ramifications, exacerbating existing difficulties associated with a personality disorder. Stigma can manifest itself in comments, blame, contradictory assumptions, and discrimination, causing a person who has a personality disorder to feel ashamed and hide their suffering. This results in more negative emotions, such as guilt, loneliness, and anxiety, and suppresses distress.

Emotional Dysregulation

Emotionally dysregulated thinking behavior is all common outcomes of suppressing distress and self-invalidation. If someone is motivated enough to fight past the stigma and seek therapy, they may face even greater stigma due to their actions. Even when a person fits diagnostic criteria, a minority of mental health practitioners are hesitant, if not outright unwilling, to diagnose and treat a personality disorder.

4.4 Screening for Borderline Personality Disorder

The diagnosis of a borderline personality problem cannot be made using a specific test; nevertheless, mental health practitioners often utilize screening tools to assist them in identifying a specific diagnosis. Here are a few examples of popular screening instruments that may be used to diagnose a personality disorder.

The McLean Screening Instrument

It is a screening tool developed by the McLean Institute. This instrument for BPD is a ten-item test frequently used to screen. Developed as a very short paper and pencil exam to identify potential personality disorders in individuals seeking treatment or who have a history of therapy, this measure was designed to be as accurate as feasible. Dr. Mary and her co-workers at the hospital were responsible for the development of this tool.

Scoring

The BPD screening test consists of ten questions based on the DSM of mental disorders diagnostic criteria for the condition. The first 8 questions of the MSI-BPD correspond to the first 8 DSM-5 diagnostic criteria for this disorder, whereas the last 2 items evaluate the final DSM-5 criterion, i.e., the paranoia or disengagement criterion, are included in the assessment. Then it is scored on a curve.

It is necessary to evaluate each item on a scale of one to ten, whether it is present or missing, and the items are totaled to get a score that may range from zero to one hundred. Having a score of seven or above means you are more likely to fulfill the criteria for borderline personality disorder.

Clinical Interview using a Structured Approach

Even though it is an update of the structured clinical discussion for DSM personality disorders, this official clinical examination of the APA is remarkably comparable to that interview. You may be asked questions directly relevant to the criteria for a personality disorder stated in the DSM-5 by your mental health professional while using this screening tool to determine your diagnosis.

It's also included an optional self-reporting form with 100 items, although it is not used by all physicians.

PDQ-4

This screening test consists of ninety-nine true or false questions to screen for various personality disorders, including borderline personality disorders.

Zanarini Scale of Evaluation

Doctors utilize this tool for diagnosing borderline personality disorder, which was also created by Dr. Mary, to assess patients who have previously been diagnosed with this disorder to determine whether or not there has been a change over time in their symptoms.

A recent study conducted with adolescents and young adults using the first three screening methods revealed that the screening instruments were equally effective in performing a personality disorder diagnosis.

4.5 In what ways does untreated Borderline Personality Disorder damage one's health?

If left untreated, the mental health disorder can manifest itself in various ways, including difficulties in daily relationships and potentially dangerous health situations. It is a mental illness characterized by mood swings and self-image issues that, if left untreated, can lead to impulsive behaviors and relationship difficulties, among other serious health problems. It is most commonly diagnosed in young women in their teen or early adult years, and it is more common in people who have experienced childhood trauma or abuse.

4.6 Difficulties in diagnosing BPD

Despite specific symptoms, a borderline personality disorder can be difficult to diagnose, like other personality disorders. Psychologists claim that this is partially attributable to a lack of comprehension. Personality disorders are not discussed enough, and they can be confusing to some people, resulting in many people who have a personality disorder not realizing they have the disorder. Other times, a patient experiencing the symptoms associated with this disorder may be ashamed to acknowledge that anything is wrong. Because it is classified as a personality problem, this disease has received a great deal of stigma.

The problem is that the name is misleading. When you refer to it as a personality disorder, it leads people to believe that it is not biologically driven. Studies claim that there are biological underpinnings to the phenomenon. Genetics, brain structure, and a history of traumatic events all play a role in determining whether or not someone is at risk for developing it. Finally, according to research, it is often misdiagnosed as bipolar since certain symptoms are similar, mainly unpredictable moods between the two conditions. In addition, according to Doctors, it can take up to five encounters with the mental health system before borderline personality disorder is identified as the source of the problem.

4.7 Serious Consequences of untreated Borderline Personality Disorder

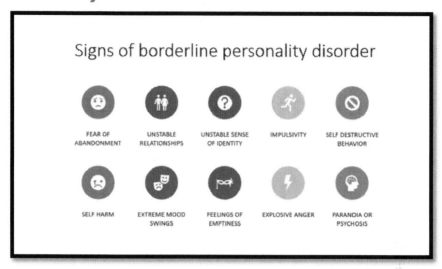

Perhaps someone is exhibiting borderline personality disorder symptoms but is either in denial or has made the conscious decision not to seek treatment. As this individual progresses through life, he or she may encounter the following situations:

Relationship Problems

People suffering from it have a black-and-white perspective on the world. When it comes to things and people, they are either good or terrible, and the emotions of someone suffering from it may shift practically quickly. Relationships, in particular, may be difficult to navigate. Individuals who have this personality disorder often have a love-hate relationship with others.

A person who has this disorder may one day consider their spouse, friend, or family member to be the greatest person on the planet. The following day, he or she may do a complete turn and declare that the greatest person on the planet is now the worst person on the planet. Some may be attributed to individuals suffering from this disorder having a strong fear of being abandoned. For example, if they believe they are in danger of being abandoned by a loved one, they may choose to break off contact with them. This may, of course, result in a great deal of interpersonal conflict and persistent problems in partnerships. Thus, individuals suffering from it are more likely than the general population to experience marital instability, divorce, and difficulty maintaining good connections with family and friends.

Work Problems

These interpersonal problems may also have a negative impact on someone's ability to keep stable employment, for example, if they have a love-hate relationship with their employer or colleagues. Symptoms of BPD may be severe and debilitating, to the point that being unable to control emotions will almost definitely destroy a person's life. What you begin to witness is a life that can only be characterized as unstable. However, this does not imply that everyone suffering from it will fall into this category. Some individuals with this personality disorder can operate very effectively. It is not inferred that a person would be unable to work or get married because of cancer. However, if the relationship issues get serious, the employee may lose his or her job.

Hospitalization as a result of self-harm

Many individuals with borderline personality disorder hurt themselves to cope with their emotions, such as through cutting. Some people may even try to end their own life, as well. Suicide attempts are so frequent among individuals with such a disorder that they are signs of the condition.

According to a study conducted by experts at Washington, up to 10 percent of individuals who meet the criteria for borderline personality disorder die by suicide, more than 50 times the risk for the general population. In most cases, this self-destructive conduct manifests itself when a person's mood is depressed. Self-mutilation and careless conduct are a result of these experiences.

According to research, the overpowering nature of suicidal thoughts may prompt someone who has this personality disorder to seek therapy in a hospital or at an inpatient treatment facility. In many cases, this kind of conduct acts as a wake-up call for the individual experiencing difficulties. For many people, the suicide attempt shocks them and makes them realize how dangerous this is to their lives.

Uncontrollable desire to engage in risky behavior.

Another consequence of borderline disorder is the tendency to engage in hazardous and irresponsible conduct. If left untreated, a person suffering from it may engage in unnecessary spending, drug abuse, binge eating, reckless driving, and violent sex with others. Impulsive conduct is often associated with the low self-esteem that many patients suffer with.

In addition to the physiological and physical consequences of participating in these hazardous activities, the person with this disorder will have to deal with the emotional and psychological consequences. For example, binge eating may result in severe health problems such as heart disease and blood sugar surges, while unsafe sex can result in sexually transmitted illnesses or unintended pregnancies.

Uncertainty and a general sense of unease

Living with a borderline personality disorder without therapy is like attempting to walk on ice without slipping. A person who has this disorder feels like this nearly all of the time, like they can't seem to get their feet under them, adds the expert. For example, individuals suffering from it may be obsessed with the fear of abandonment, whether real or imagined, as was stated previously. They may also have a distorted perception of reality, believing that they are cut off from themselves and see their own body from the outside.

According to the NIMH, individuals who have this disorder and refuse treatment are at risk of developing additional physical problems and mental disorders in the future. According to research, about 10 percent of individuals with it also have bipolar illness, and another 10 percent of people with it also have bipolar two disorder. It may seem odd that having one personality disorder increases the likelihood of getting another, yet this is true throughout the spectrum of personality disorders. Those who have personality disorders are at a higher risk of developing additional anxiety, attitude, and impulse control difficulties, as well as drug addiction problems.

4.8 Dual Diagnosis of Bipolar disorder and Borderline Personality Disorder

Bipolar disorder is a general term that refers to mood disorders marked by extreme swings in mood. It is possible to go from manic or hypomanic high emotions to depressed, low moods while experiencing mood swings. A personality disorder is characterized by volatility in one's behavior, functioning, mood, and self-image. In many ways, bipolar illness and borderline disorders are the same things; they seem different. This is especially true in type 1 bipolar disorder, which is characterized by severe manic episodes.

> The following are some symptoms that are common to both bipolar disorder and borderline personality disorder:
>
> - Emotional outbursts to the extreme
>
> - Acts have taken on the spur of the moment
>
> - Suicidal thoughts and actions

Some believe that bipolar disease is a subset of the bipolar spectrum. The majority of specialists, on the other hand, believe that the two diseases are distinct. According to a study on the connection between borderline personality disorder and bipolar disorder, about 20 percent of individuals with type 2 bipolar disorder are diagnosed with a personality disorder.

A personality disorder diagnosis is given to about 10 percent of individuals who have type 1 bipolar illness. A comprehensive examination of the diseases is necessary for accurate differentiation. This may assist in determining if you have one condition with inclinations toward the other disorder or whether you have both disorders simultaneously.

When a person has both diseases, what symptoms do they experience?

When a person has both disorders, they will exhibit symptoms specific to each disease.

The following are symptoms that are specific to bipolar disorder:

- Highly euphoric emotions characterize manic episodes

- Signs and symptoms of depression.

- Sleep alterations in both amount and quality are seen.

Among the symptoms that are specific to a borderline personality disorder are:

- Emotional shifts occur daily as a result of variables such as family and job stress.

- Relationships that are strong and have trouble controlling emotions.

- Cutting, hurting, striking, or harming oneself are all examples of self-harm signs and symptoms.

- Emotions of emptiness or boredom that last for a long time.

- Outbursts of strong, often uncontrolled rage are almost always followed by emotions of shame or remorse.

What is the best way to get a diagnosis for both conditions?

Most individuals who have a dual diagnosis of these illnesses get one diagnosis before the other. This is because the symptoms of one disease may overlap and even disguise the symptoms of another. Because the symptoms of bipolar illness may vary, it is frequently the first disease to be identified. This makes it more difficult to recognize the signs and symptoms of borderline personality disorder. With time and therapy for one condition, the other may become more apparent.

If you suspect that you are suffering from bipolar illness or a personality disorder, schedule an appointment with your doctor and describe your symptoms. To establish the type and degree of your symptoms, they will most likely evaluate you. Your doctor will consult the DSM of mental disorders to assist them in making a diagnosis. They will go over each of your symptoms to see if they are consistent with the other condition.

In addition, your doctor will take into account your mental health history. Often, this can provide insight that can aid in the differentiation of one disorder from the other. For example, these problems are more likely to run in families. This means that if you have a close relative who suffers from one or both of the disorders, you are more likely to develop them yourself as well.

What is the treatment approach for bipolar disorder and bipolar disorder with psychosis?

The therapies for these disorders are distinct since each disease manifests differently.

Bipolar illness necessitates several different kinds of therapy, including:
• Mood stabilizers, Antipsychotics, Antidepressants, and Anti-anxiety medicines are examples of pharmaceuticals that may be prescribed.
• Talk therapy, family therapy, and group therapy are all examples of this.
• Treatments that are not conventional. Among these options is electroconvulsive treatment.
• Medications for sleep. Depending on the severity of the symptoms, your doctor may recommend sleep medicines.

Typically, talk therapy is used to treat bipolar personality disorder, and it is the same kind of treatment that may be used to treat this disorder.

However, your doctor may also recommend the following:
• Treatment based on dialectic behavior.
• Therapy that is centered on schemas.
• Treatment based on cognitive-behavioral principles

> - Developing emotional predictability and problem-solving skills through systems training.

Experts do not suggest that individuals with borderline disorder utilize medication as their main therapy. Medicine may exacerbate symptoms, particularly suicidal inclinations. However, a doctor may prescribe medicines to address certain mood swings or sadness in certain cases.

In certain cases, hospitalization may be required for the treatment of both diseases. When the manic episodes associated with bipolar illness are coupled with the suicidal inclinations triggered by BPD, a person can attempt suicide. If you have both diseases, you should abstain from consuming alcoholic beverages and using illegal substances. These illnesses enhance a person's likelihood of engaging in drug addiction, which may exacerbate their symptoms.

> Suicide prevention is important. If you believe someone is in imminent danger of self-harm or harming another person, take the following steps:
>
> - Call 911 or the appropriate emergency number in your area.
> - Keep an eye on the individual until assistance comes.
> - Remove any weapons, blades, medicines, or other items that may be used to hurt someone.

- Listen without interjecting with judgment, argument, threat, or yelling.

What is the prognosis for someone who has been diagnosed with both conditions?

A combined diagnosis of both disorders may occasionally result in severe symptoms. The individual may need intensive inpatient treatment in a hospital environment. In other instances, individuals who suffer from both illnesses may need outpatient treatment rather than hospitalization. Every aspect of the situation is dependent on the degree and intensity of both diseases.

One of the diseases may be producing more severe symptoms than the other. Both of these disorders with psychosis are long-term illnesses. When dealing with any of these illnesses, it is critical to collaborate with your doctor to create a treatment plan that is effective for you. This will help to guarantee that your symptoms improve rather than worsen in the future. If you believe your therapy isn't working as well, you should speak with your doctor as soon as possible about it.

05

Living With Borderline Personality Disorder

Identity disturbance is a phrase that refers to incoherence or inconsistency in a person's perception of who they are or what

they want to be. This may imply that a person's objectives, views, and behaviors are continuously shifting and evolving. Alternatively, the individual may adopt the personality characteristics of others around them as they battle to establish and preserve their sense of self.

5.1 Self-doubt and Identity disturbance

According to the manual, the DSM defines identity disturbance as a markedly and consistently unstable self-image or sense of self, and it is one of the main symptoms of this personality disorder. Of course, individuals who do not have a personality disorder also suffer from identity instability. On the other hand, people suffering from it often suffer from a severe loss of sense of self, also known as identity loss. If you are struggling with the sensation that you have no clue who you are or what you believe in, this may be a symptom that you can identify with.

Understanding one's own Identity

A person's identity is often considered as their overall perception and perspective of themselves. A solid sense of identity refers to perceiving oneself as the same person in the past, present, and future. It is important to maintain this ability. Furthermore, maintaining a stable sense of self requires the capacity to see yourself in the same light even though you may behave in conflicting ways from time to time. Identity is a wide concept that encompasses many different elements of one's personality.

The following components are considered to be part of your sense of self or your identity:
• Your views
• Your methods of acting
• Your beliefs and attitudes
• Your assessment of your skills
• The social roles that you play
• Your personality and temperament

Identity may be regarded as your self-definition; it is the glue that binds all of these disparate parts of your personality together as a whole.

Why is it Important to have a Unique Identity?

Having a strong sense of one's own identity serves a variety of purposes. A strong sense of self may assist you in adapting to new situations. The world around you is always changing, but when you have a strong sense of self, you have an anchor that may help you stay afloat as you make the transition. The absence of such a foundation may make changes seem chaotic and even frightening. In addition, having a strong sense of self helps you to build your self-confidence. How can you create a feeling that you are valuable and deserving of respect if you don't know who you are?

Signs and Symptoms

Identity disturbance is also referred to as identity dispersion in certain circles. Problems are identifying who you are in connection to other people while you are experiencing this. Some individuals with this disorder may have difficulty knowing where they begin and the other person ends. People who have a personality disorder often claim no clue who they are or what they believe in. They have said that they sometimes feel as though they are just non-existent. People have even said that they are similar to a chameleon when it comes to their identity, changing who they are based on their surroundings and what they believe others expect of them.

It is possible to be the life of the party at social gatherings while maintaining a solemn attitude at business occasions, for example. Although everyone's conduct varies in various situations, those with borderline personality disorder see a much greater fluctuation in their behavior. Patients with identity disruption are more prone to have contradictory beliefs and actions, and they may tend to over-identify with groups or positions at the expense of their unique personalities. Many individuals with borderline personality disorder (BPD) report that their thoughts and emotions shift to fit the present circumstances and alter their conduct.

In the case of the following, people may often alter their views regarding the following:
• Their friendships
• Their aspirations
• Their professional lives
• Their points of view and values
• Other significant life choices

Consequently, many individuals who have borderline personality disorder find it difficult to establish and maintain appropriate personal boundaries, and they have problems in their interpersonal and intimate relationships. They may also have difficulty making long-term commitments to beliefs, objectives, and employment.

5.2 Relationship Issues in Borderline Personality Disorder

Patients with BPD who struggle with identity instability often have difficulty establishing intimate connections with other individuals. Someone suffering from identity disturbance is likely to suffer from the negative consequences of poor self-esteem, such as a lack of self-respect and a lack of personal boundaries.

Another difficulty in maintaining healthy connections for those who suffer from identity disturbance is the lack of support or meaninglessness in their interactions. Those suffering from identity disturbance are prone to experiencing an emptiness on the inside. Because it is difficult for them to find meaning inside themselves, they may have difficulty finding meaning in their connections with their families, colleagues, and love partners as a result.

Causes

There has been relatively little study on the identity issues linked with a personality disorder, but there are many ideas why individuals with it often struggle with their identities. For example, a prominent researcher in this personality disorder and the creator of dialectical therapy thinks that you create an identity through monitoring your own emotions, opinions, and experiences, as well as the responses of others to you.

Many individuals with this disorder originate from chaotic or abusive environments, contributing to their fragile sense of self.

Suppose you decide who you are based on people's responses to you, and those reactions have been unexpected and frightening. In that case, you will have no foundation for establishing a strong sense of personal identity in the future. Mentalizing is a term used to describe the capacity to comprehend the mental states of oneself and others. This is particularly challenging for those who suffer from identity instability and a personality disorder.

In other words, they have difficulty understanding and anticipating human behavior and intentions, making it even more difficult for them to get to know themselves and others intimately. According to research, it has been suggested that this difficulty with mentalizing may be a contributing factor to why individuals with it suffer so much with identity dissemination and interpersonal connections.

5.3 How to Find your Inner self and Tackle these Problems?

So, what is the best way to respond to the question? What exactly am I? Of course, there is no magic answer to the issue of the identity. On the other hand, contain components that may assist you in discovering who you are and what you stand for in your life. Often, the first step is locating a qualified therapist who can assist you in dealing with identity issues.

Treatments for a personality disorder that may be effective in alleviating identity disruption include:
• **Cognitive-behavioral therapy:** This kind of treatment may assist a person in identifying any limiting ideas that they may have about themselves or others, making it simpler over time to establish connections with others. It also treats the underlying causes of anxiety and depressive symptoms.
• **Dialectical behavior therapy:** This treatment assists a person in coping with strong emotions and gaining control over harmful conduct. In it, mindfulness is a strategy that is often used.
• **Therapy based on mentalization:** a therapist helps a person with borderline personality disorder develop their interpersonal abilities. This kind of treatment is intended to help them better understand what they and others are thinking or experiencing, among other things.
• **Transference-focused therapy:** When a client interacts with their therapist, elements of their identity disturbance manifest themselves in the treatment relationship in many ways they would with

> a friend or family member in their daily lives. This offers a means for the therapist to assist the patient in integrating many parts of his or herself.
>
> - **Schema-focused therapy:** It is a type of psychotherapy that integrates various psychotherapeutic techniques to assist patients in changing entrenched patterns or schemas that may contribute to identity challenges.

Additionally, there are methods for dealing with identity disruption that you may do on your own. You may begin to understand what is important to you in your life and what you consider to be significant. When used in combination with therapy, this kind of self-discovery may be most helpful, particularly for individuals who suffer from identity disturbance, who often struggle to find purpose in their lives. Finding out what's most important to you may help you develop a stronger sense of your own identity.

5.4 Self- Mutilation

Unless you have personally experienced the desire to participate in this mutilation, it may be extremely difficult to comprehend what others are going through. A friend or family member who has a personality disorder and self-mutilates may be terrifying, perplexing, and upsetting for everyone involved. Understanding why someone engages in it may assist you in assisting your loved one in coping with these impulses and acting as a support network for that person.

What is the meaning of Self-Mutilation?

It is defined as the intentional and direct damage or modification of one's own body by oneself. Cutting, burning, hitting oneself with needles, and extreme scratching are all examples of these behaviors. Non-suicidal self-injury is a phrase that is often used in the study. When compared to other forms of self-harming behavior, it is typically very distinct.

People who harm themselves are not generally intending to kill themselves, as shown by research, but some may express ambivalence regarding the motivation behind their actions. Those who do it are not always suicidal; many of those who have suicidal thoughts and have even attempted suicide at some point in their lives. In addition, individuals have died as a result of their injuries in instances of very severe self-mutilation.

Why do people do Self-Mutilation?

Self-Mutilation is done for a variety of reasons. Many people think that individuals do it to attract attention. This is a fallacy. The majority of individuals who self-harm do it in secret, and they take care to conceal any signs or scars that result. Self-harmers will often wear long sleeves to conceal these indications of distress.

They are most likely embarrassed by their actions and want to keep them hidden. Those who have borderline personality disorder who are sensitive to rejection, in particular, are always concerned about others finding out what they are hiding from them. Several studies have shown that most individuals manage internal experiences such as strong emotions, thoughts, memories, and physical sensations, among other things.

Who does Self-Mutilation?

Unfortunately, it is a frequent occurrence, especially among individuals who have a borderline disorder. One study discovered that insecure attachment, childhood separation, emotional negligence, and sexual abuse and dissociation were significant risk factors for self-injury among college students (not necessarily those with this disorder). The study also discovered that the risk factors were gender-specific.

Evidence indicates substantial variations between men and women regarding the incidence of self-harm, the technique used, and the location of harm on the body. Compared to men, women reported higher rates of activity overall, greater amounts of cutting and scratching, and more harm to arms and legs. Men reported greater self-hitting and burning and more injury to their chests, faces, and genitals than women.

Similarly, in another research of children in the third, sixth, and ninth grades in one community, six ninth-grade females were shown to be the most at risk, with a similar injury pattern of greater cutting and scratching, and engaged in self-harm three times more often than boys. People who have suffered maltreatment during their childhood, such as sexual abuse or neglect, or who have been removed from a caregiver throughout their childhood are more likely than the general population to engage in self-mutilation later in life.

Treatment for self-mutilation

It is often used to cope with strong emotions. Cognitive-behavioral therapies are geared at assisting the individual in developing new, better methods of managing emotions and thoughts. For example, DBT or CBT for this personality disorder tackles harmful efforts at coping by assisting the patient in learning and practicing a new set of coping skills. When necessary, a doctor may give medicines to manage emotions and moods while also reducing the desire to commit self-harm in certain instances.

Speaking with a friend or loved one about self-mutilation should be done in a non-judgmental manner if you want to help them stop. It is possible to make someone feel heard and understood by approaching them gently and carefully. Before speaking with a loved one, it may be beneficial to contact a therapist specializing in treating a personality disorder and mutilation. He can provide you with expert guidance on how to handle the issue in the most effective manner without scaring or upsetting your loved one.

5.5 Splitting and Borderline Personality Disorder

Splitting is a psychiatric word that refers to the inability to

simultaneously retain two conflicting ideas, emotions, or beliefs. According to those who divide their views, the world is seen as black or white, everything or nothing. It is a skewed style of thinking in which the good or negative characteristics of a person or event are neither evaluated nor considered in conjunction with one another. According to experts, those with this personality disorder use splitting as a defensive strategy, allowing them to see people, situations, and even themselves in an all-or-nothing manner. It enables individuals to quickly reject things they have labeled as bad and embrace those they deem excellent, even if those items are damaging or dangerous.

Effects of Splitting Behavior

It is possible to split apart and engage in severe and self-destructive conduct, which may cause problems in relationships. A person who divides will usually frame individuals or situations in absolute terms, with little room for negotiation or compromise amid the conversation.

The following are examples of splitting behavior:
• Opportunities may either be risk-free or completely dishonest.
• Individuals can either be evil and corrupt or angel and perfect.
• When things go wrong, a person will feel deceived, broken, or screwed.

What makes it even more difficult to understand is that the belief may sometimes be unwavering while at other times shifting back and forth from one instant to the next. People who break up are often seen as excessively theatrical or overdone, particularly when they declare that things have totally come apart or fully turned around, respectively. Such conduct may be tiring for people who are near it.

Symptoms

Splitting may seem to be a frequent occurrence in and of itself, a behavior that can be ascribed to any number of people we know, including ourselves.

On the other hand, it is regarded to be a persistent and distorted behavior in borderline disorder, and it is typically accompanied by additional symptoms such as:

- Putting up a show, acting without consideration to consequences.

- Denial of the facts, consciously ignoring a fact or reality.

- Emotions trigger hypochondriasis. Trying to get others to understand how severe your emotional pain is.

- The ability to do anything at any time. The belief that you possess superiority in intelligence or power.

- Aggression in a passive manner, an indirect expression of hostility.

- Projection is a term that refers to the act of projecting something into the future, assigning an undesirable emotion to someone else.

- Identification is based on projections, denying your feelings, projecting them onto someone else, and then behaving toward that person in a way that forces them to respond to you with the feelings you projected onto them.

Diagnosis and Management of the Condition

When it comes to an understanding borderline disorder, knowing the diagnostic process and the careful treatment of the illness may be beneficial in understanding behaviors such as splitting that are linked with the condition.

Specifically, the clinician would need to confirm five of the nine symptoms included in the DSM/5 to establish the diagnosis.

These symptoms include:
• Feeling persistently empty or bored.
• A distorted self-perception that impacts your sentiments, values, feelings, and interpersonal interactions.
• Temper issues, such as severe disturbances followed by intense guilt and shame.
• Extreme efforts to withdraw abandonment or extreme feelings of abandonment.
• Extreme sadness, fear, or anger can last for hours or days.
• Feeling dissociated from yourself, including paranoia and amnesia.
• Impulsive behavior, such as abusing substances or engaging in risky sexual behavior

There is no simple solution, particularly severe symptoms, when dealing with a loved one who has this borderline personality disorder. The type of connection and the effect your loved one's symptoms have on your family will significantly influence how you deal with the situation.

However, certain guiding concepts may be useful, such as the following:

- Develop a strong sense of empathy. As a starting point, remind yourself that splitting is an aspect of your condition. Your loved one is not acting in a malicious or manipulative manner, even though some behaviors may seem to be deliberate or manipulative. These are merely defensive strategies that individuals use anytime they feel helpless or unprotected.

- Encouraging and assisting with therapy your loved one may have a better life if they get treatment, which may involve medication and talk therapy, the most probable of which will be dialectical behavioral therapy.

- Would you please encourage them to begin or continue with therapy and learn all they can about what they are going through to be supportive? Participate in treatment sessions with your loved one if it is necessary.

- Keep the lines of communication open and accessible. When you discuss a problem as soon as it occurs, you can isolate that occurrence rather than stacking one scenario on top of another. If you don't communicate, you'll simply help to exacerbate your loved one's rejection anxieties.

- Remind your loved ones that you are thinking about them. People who have a personality disorder are often afraid of being rejected or abandoned. Remembering that someone is concerned about you regularly may assist in decreasing your splitting behavior.

- Define your limits. Dealing with the difficulties of BPD is one thing; being the target of abuse is quite another. Always establish boundaries with a loved one who suffers from it. If you find yourself on the wrong side of that boundary, explain why you are backing away as objectively as possible. Setting limits rather than questioning the connection helps to keep the partnership together.

- Take good care of your physical and mental health. This may include hiring your therapist to assist you in

> finding a way to balance your demands with those of your loved one.

> • Make an effort to keep your reaction under control. Keep in mind that if your loved one suffers from this disorder, you are in a better position to maintain control over your emotions. Using profanity or displaying animosity will only help to exacerbate the current issue more.

There may be instances when you'll need to take more extreme measures to protect yourself. If your connection is causing damage to your family, your job, and your overall feeling of well-being, you may have to confront the fact that the relationship cannot be maintained. While this is a difficult decision for everyone concerned, it may also be the most beneficial in certain circumstances. This choice should be made with the assistance of a competent mental health practitioner, if at all possible.

5.6 Regulation of Emotions in People with Borderline Personality Disorder

Most individuals with personality disorder experience strong emotions and have difficulty controlling these feelings. It is believed that emotional dysregulation is a fundamental symptom of personality disorder and that it may explain other features of the disease, such as unstable relationships, hazardous or impulsive conduct, and stress-related changes in thinking. Emotional instability is also included in the diagnostic criteria for this disorder.

What is Emotional Regulation, and How does it work?

One of the most difficult aspects of emotional regulation is the mix of ways in which a person responds to and acts on emotional events.

Among these skills include the capacity to:
• Respond properly when disturbed.
• Recognize, comprehend, and accept emotional experiences.
• Employ healthy coping methods to deal with unpleasant emotions.

Those skilled in emotion regulation can resist the temptation to participate in impulsive actions such as self-harm, reckless conduct, or physical violence while under emotional stress or anxiety. Emotional control abilities are learned and developed throughout the early childhood years. Our development includes learning techniques to help us comprehend what we're experiencing and self-soothe when we're upset.

Several factors may have a detrimental effect on this process, including:
• Dissimilarities in brain anatomy.
• Parents who are harsh or overbearing.

- A lack of a solid connection to one's parents.

- Stress or trauma experienced throughout childhood.

Emotional regulation vs. Emotional dysregulation

While emotion regulation helps us deal with setbacks, someone who suffers from emotion dysregulation will have difficulty understanding their emotions and healthily reacting to them. This is particularly important in this disorder since individuals suffering from the disease often feel considerable discomfort when confronted with emotionally charged circumstances. Our ability to regulate our emotions has a significant impact on how we react to certain situations in our daily lives.

For example, suppose someone with emotion management abilities has a breakup. In that case, they will certainly feel sad and perhaps a little depressed, but they will be able to maintain control over their feelings and continue with their regular activities. Someone who has it may, on the other hand, become depressed to the point of being unable to function. To cope, they may resort to destructive or aggressive conduct, as well as impulsive hobbies like promiscuity and gambling.

5.7 Borderline Personality Disorder and Emotional Issues

People who have this disorder have various symptoms linked to their ability to control their emotions. As a result of these factors, people may have substantial difficulties in their everyday lives by experiencing anxiety and depression, finding it difficult to establish solid relationships, or experiencing difficulties at work. People with this disorder may also engage in impulsive, self-destructive, or even harmful activities to deal with their emotional dysregulation. Irritability and rapid mood swings are two symptoms of this disorder.

Mood Swings

People with this personality disorder have difficulty controlling their moods and expressing their feelings, resulting in anxiety and irritation. Mood swings may be both strong and fast in their progression. These emotions of worry and irritation may interfere with your ability to do daily tasks such as working at a job or even caring for yourself. Others may find it difficult to be around you during these periods for various reasons, which may have a negative impact on your relationships.

When it comes to individuals with borderline disorder, emotional sensitivity may be the driving force behind their mood swings and anger. Generally speaking, someone suffering from this disease is more emotionally sensitive than the average person, leading them to respond rapidly and strongly to the circumstances they are presented with.

Difficulty in maintaining control over Anger

Along with extreme mood swings comes a burst of rage that seems to appear out of nowhere. Even the smallest annoyance may cause anger in those who have a personality disorder, which can escalate to destructive or violent conduct, including self-harm, in some cases. Problems in emotion regulation seem to be strongly associated with difficulties in controlling rage. The intensity and stability may also play a part in this, as individuals in unstable, chaotic relationships may be more prone to displaying violent behaviors.

Emptiness

Those who have borderline personality disorder often have a persistent sense of emptiness. While it is not quite obvious where this sensation originates from, it may be linked to a negative self-image. Someone suffering from it may find it difficult to maintain a clear sense of their own identity, and they may feel detached from both themselves and others. This sense of emptiness is very disruptive, and it may lead to impulsive actions, such as self-harm and suicide, as well as other negative consequences. It may also lead to loneliness since someone suffering from chronic emptiness may feel detached from others and find it difficult to sustain connections. You may find it difficult to control your emotions if you are experiencing this isolation, which may set off a vicious cycle that exacerbates your feelings of sadness and exhaustion.

Paranoia and the Fear of Being Abandoned

People with this personality disorder are often frightened of being alone, rejected, or abandoned by people closest to them, leading to severe paranoia. If they feel rejected in the future, they may behave compulsively and seek reassurance all the time, or they may push people away to prevent feeling hurt again. The unfortunate reality is that many of these habits may contribute to a lack of solid partnerships. This may be exacerbated if you have difficulty controlling your emotions. People may become more distant if they have frequent, intense emotional outbursts. If you cannot calm emotions of paranoia or insecurity, this may lead to greater instability in your relationships.

Managing Emotions despite BPD

If you are struggling with borderline personality disorder and emotion regulation, you may want to explore visiting a therapist who is trained in this area. They will have a greater knowledge of the roots of your emotional problems, and you may work together to develop methods to assist you in learning how to control your emotions and manage your mood swings more effectively.

Dialectical behavior therapy is a treatment created especially to assist individuals who have a personality disorder in learning how to alter their ideas and actions, thus alleviating the symptoms of the illness.

In addition to treatment, several self-help techniques for this personality disorder may help you improve your capacity to control your emotions even more effectively.

These can include:
• Engaging in regular physical activity.
• Engaging in mindfulness meditation.
• Expressing your emotions through writing.
• Educating yourself about this personality disorder.
• Employing grounding techniques during intense distress.
• Incorporating stress-reduction techniques into your daily routine.

06

Medications for Borderline Personality Disorder

It is necessary to treat borderline personality disorder throughout a person's life since it is a chronic disease. People

who have many bouts of mood shifts in a year (four or more episodes) may considerably be more difficult to manage. Although medication is the main

mode of treatment, psychotherapy is occasionally prescribed to help avoid recurrent attacks. There are a wide variety of medications available to treat this illness.

Proposed treatment choices are based on the three primary stages of this disorder: acute manic mood states, major depressive episodes, and ultimately the continuation phase.

The use of two mood stabilizers in combination with antidepressants is a successful approach for most patients.

6.1 Reasons for taking Medications

Individuals who have BPD may want to experiment with medication to treat their condition for various reasons. The essential thing to remember is always collaborating with your doctor to identify which pharmaceutical choices may be appropriate for you, depending on your symptoms and requirements.

Some of the reasons why you may wish to try these medicines are as follows:
• **Decrease the intensity of symptoms:** Medications may be used to assist individuals in better control some of the symptoms of BPD, such as mood swings, irritability, sadness, anxiety, and stress-related paranoia.
• **Increase the effectiveness of treatment:** Due to the medication's ability to alleviate certain symptoms, it may also be possible to enhance a person's functioning in various areas, including relationships and everyday activities.
• **Prevent the worsening of symptoms:** Because certain borderline personality disorder symptoms may

increase if left untreated, using medication to alleviate those symptoms may be beneficial.

- **Improve the quality of life:** By research findings, the frequency and severity of borderline disorder symptoms tend to decrease as individuals become older.

- **Take care of any co-occurring conditions:** This personality disorder often co-occurs with other disorders that may interact with one another, overlap, and make it more difficult to diagnose this personality disorder properly. Depression, anxiety complications, eating disorders, drug use disorders, and bipolar disorder are among illnesses that often co-occur with a borderline personality disorder.

- **Reduced risk of suicide:** This disorder is linked with an increased risk of self-harm and suicide, among other things. Because medicines may decrease the frequency and intensity of symptoms, they may also minimize the chance of committing suicide.

6.2 Types of Borderline Personality Disorder Medications

Although no drug is specifically designed to treat borderline personality disorder, many pharmaceuticals may help treat distinct symptoms of the condition. The kind of medicine that your doctor recommends will be determined by the particular symptoms and requirements that you present.

Antidepressants

They were created especially for treating people suffering from major depressive disorder and other illnesses characterized by depressed mood. However, these medicines are used to treat a large number of individuals with a borderline personality disorder

. It has been shown that several kinds of these antidepressants are used to treat BPD, such as:

- Tricyclic antidepressants
- Tetracyclic antidepressants
- Monoamine oxidase inhibitors
- Selective serotonin reuptake inhibitors

Common antidepressants include:

- Zoloft (Sertraline)
- Nardil (Phenelzine)
- Effexor (Venlafaxine)
- Prozac (Fluoxetine)
- Wellbutrin (Bupropion)

These medicines may alleviate symptoms such as sadness, low mood, anxiety, and impulsive reactivity, but they do not seem to have a significant impact on the majority of other symptoms (e.g., agitation, impulsivity).

Antipsychotics

Early psychiatrists thought that the symptoms of this personality disorder were on the boundary between obsession and psychosis, hence coining the name borderline. As a result, these medicines were among the first medicines to be investigated for this personality disorder. These medications are also effective in the treatment of several non-psychotic illnesses. These medications have been proven to decrease symptoms of this borderline disorder, such as stress, neurotic thinking, anger, resentment, and impulsivity.

The following are examples of common antipsychotic medicines:
• Aripiprazole
• Geodon (Ziprasidone)
• Seroquel (Quetiapine)
• Risperdal (Risperidone)
• Zyprexa (olanzapine)

Mood Stabilizers

Lithium and certain anticonvulsant medicines have been used to treat impulsive behavior and rapid changes in emotion linked with this borderline personality disorder.

There is evidence to indicate that certain types of medications may be beneficial in the treatment of it.
• Depakote (Valproate)
• Lamictal (lamotrigine)
• Lithobid (Lithium carbonate)
• Tegretol (Carbamazepine)

Anxiolytics

They are the medications that relieve anxiety. Because people with borderline personality disorder are also prone to experiencing severe anxiety, medicines to alleviate this condition are often given. Unfortunately, there is very little evidence to support the use of anti-anxiety medications to treat it.

Anxiolytics mostly prescribed are:
• Ativan (Lorazepam)
• Xanax (Alprazolam)
• Valium (Diazepam)

• Klonopin (Clonazepam)
• Buspar (Buspirone)

Certain research suggests that using a specific type of anxiolytics, benzodiazepines (e.g., ativan and klonopin), may exacerbate symptoms in some people with a borderline personality disorder. They should only be prescribed under strict supervision. Because they can become habit-forming, benzodiazepines are especially hazardous when used by people with co-occurring drug use disorders. It is possible to use Buspar as an alternative to medicines from this family since it is non-addictive and does not cause dependence.

Anticonvulsants

Lithium is a medication that helps to stabilize one's mood. It is effective in the treatment of mania and depression and the prevention of depression and manic episodes. It will begin to alleviate symptoms of mania within two weeks after beginning treatment, but it may take several weeks to many months until the illness is fully stabilized and under control. As a result, additional medications, such as antipsychotics or antidepressants, may be taken to manage the symptoms of schizophrenia.

The following are some of the most common lithium side effects:

- Nausea
- Weight gain
- Kidney failure
- Increased thirst
- Frequent urination
- Slight shaking of the hands

You may develop thyroid and renal issues. Your doctor will check the function of your thyroid and kidneys, in addition to the levels of lithium in your blood, which can quickly become dangerously high. Things like switching to a low-sodium diet and experiencing excessive perspiration, temperature, vomiting, or diarrhea may lead to a buildup of lithium in the body, leading to toxicity if not treated promptly. Be aware of these problems and notify your doctor immediately if you take it and develop any of these symptoms.

An overdose of lithium manifests itself in the following ways. If you notice any of the following symptoms, call your doctor or go to the closest emergency hospital right away:

- Confusion
- Convulsions

• Dizziness
• Double vision
• Severe shaking
• Unusual bruising or bleeding
• Uncontrolled eye movements
• The need to pass huge quantities of urine

Anti-seizure Medicines

Valproate is an anti-seizure medication that is also helpful in the treatment of manic episodes. It is also beneficial for individuals who suffer from borderline illness with fast cycling.

The drug has some side effects, including:
• Sedation
• Diarrhea
• Indigestion
• Nausea
• Weight gain
• Stomach cramps
• Shaking of the hands
• The possibility of liver inflammation.

- Decrease in the number of platelets.

As a result, your doctor will closely monitor your valproate levels, as well as your liver function and platelet counts.

Among the other anti-seizure medications often used to treat borderline personality disorder are:

- Carbamazepine (Tegretol)

- Lamotrigine (Lamictal)

Lamotrigine is a mood stabilizer drug that may be taken alone or in conjunction with other medications. Treating the depressive phase of this disorder and as a mood stabilizer to decrease cycling is more successful than other medications. It is a prescription medication that is available as a generic. The majority of patients report that it is well-tolerated and that there are no adverse effects.

The following are serious adverse effects of it that are reported to your doctor:

- Flu

- Rash

- Body pains

- Swollen glands

- Suicidal thoughts

- Depressive symptoms

Atypical Neuroleptics

This family of medicines, which is often referred to as antipsychotics, is also helpful in treating this illness, particularly in mania and depression.

There are many medicines in this category, including:

- Aripiprazole (Abilify)
- Olanzapine (Zyprexa)
- Lurasidone (Latuda)
- Quetiapine (Seroquel)
- Iloperidone (Fanapt)
- Ziprasidone (Geodon)
- Cariprazine (Vraylar)
- Brexpiprazole (Rexulti)

The following are some of the most common adverse effects of these medications:

- Tremors
- Muscle spasms and contractions
- Increased cholesterol levels
- Movements that are not voluntary
- Increased glucose and lipid levels
- Movements that are irregular and jerky

- Stiffness and slowness of movement

The majority of individuals who suffer from this illness take several medications. Additionally, patients may be prescribed medicine for agitation, stress, sleeplessness, or distress in addition to a mood stabilizer. Many antidepressants may be used in conjunction with these medications to treat the depression associated with borderline illness. When taken alone, it may cause a person who has this disorder to have manic symptoms.

6.3 Additional Treatment Options

Your doctor may recommend various other treatment choices, including:

- Stimulants to alleviate depression.

- Thyroid medicines to function as mood stabilizers.

- Ketamine therapy: used intravenously in conjunction with other medications has been proven effective in treating depression.

- Electroconvulsive therapy: a treatment for severe depression that involves passing an electric current through the brain.

- Transcranial magnetic stimulation: a small electromagnetic coil that passes electric current into the brain.

- The light treatment: makes use of a lightbox that emits a strong light that is comparable to that of natural sunshine. It's utilized to treat depression.

- An electrical pulse that is sent via the vegas nerve by a vagus nerve stimulator, which is a device that is implanted under the skin (a nerve that runs from the brainstem through the neck and down to each side of the chest and abdomen). The pulse is effective in the treatment of depressive symptoms.

Other Medicines

New medicines for BPD are being developed and evaluated as we understand more about the biological origins of the condition.

Researchers are investigating novel pharmaceutical alternatives for treating a personality disorder, including:
• Neuropeptide agents
• Cannabinoid medicines
• Medications that target serotonin receptors

For example, results from one research indicate that taking an omega-3 fatty acid supplement may reduce aggressiveness and feelings of anger in individuals with BPD.

Side Effects

People using medicines to treat borderline disorder may suffer side effects, just as with any other substance.

It is essential to note that each one has its unique set of adverse effects when taking medications.
• Fatigue
• Insomnia
• Nausea
• Changes in appetite.
• Constipation, diarrhea, and dry mouth.

Some individuals may also have adverse responses to the medicines they are prescribed. If you begin to develop signs of an allergic response, you should seek medical care as soon as possible. Never hesitate to inform your doctor about any adverse effects, both common and uncommon, that you are experiencing while taking a particular medicine. To prevent potentially dangerous drug interactions, it is also critical to inform your doctor of any other medicines, substances, or supplements that you are taking.

Challenges

Various difficulties may arise while using medicines to treat BPD.

These are some examples:
• **People have various requirements:** A significant degree of variability and variety is seen in the symptoms that each encounter.
• **It is usual for two or more situations to coexist,** making it more difficult to choose medicine. Antidepressants, for example, should not be taken in the presence of borderline mental illness since these medications have the potential to induce manic episodes.
• **Several methods may be required:** It is possible that medications will not be sufficient to treat all of your symptoms, so other measures like psychotherapy and self-care are necessary.

Precautions

Certain precautions should be followed before attempting to use a drug to treat borderline personality disorder.

Among the issues to consider are the following:
• People with borderline disorder should avoid using benzodiazepines because research indicates that they may exacerbate their symptoms of impulsivity and suicide ideation.
• Research indicates that individuals with BPD may be at a greater risk of developing benzodiazepine dependency due to their attempts to self-medicate.
• Antidepressants are labeled with a black-box warning on the package. This warning states that antidepressants are linked with an elevated risk of suicide ideation in adolescents and young adults.

Coping

Individuals who suffer from BPD may take steps to enhance their capacity to deal with their condition.

These are some examples:
• Treating co-occurring conditions is also essential. Treatment for borderline personality illness may be made more difficult by the presence of other mental

health problems such as drug abuse, stress disorders, depression, mental ailment, and post-traumatic stress disorder. Taking care of your co-occurring disorders may make you feel a lot better.

- Discovering effective stress management techniques is important. Stress may significantly aggravate its symptoms; therefore, identifying and implementing strategies to decrease or manage stress can benefit.

- Deep breathing, exercise, visualization, and gradual muscle relaxation are just a few of the strategies that you may wish to attempt to relax yourself.

- It is also possible to improve your everyday functioning by learning effective coping skills. For example, learning efficient methods to cope with emotional discomfort and regulate impulsive actions may help you operate better in your daily life.

- A few tools that may assist you in developing and strengthening your coping abilities include mindfulness, social support, and dialectical behavioral therapy.

07

Self-Care For People With BPD

Living with BPD may be challenging. You may come to realize that your actions and ideas are self-destructive or harmful, yet you may believe that you are unable to change them. It is recommended that you get  suitable therapy to assist you in learning new adaptive coping strategies.

7.1 Suggestions for BPD Self-care

• Follow your treatment plan.
• Attend therapy sessions regularly.
• Establish excellent and healthy habits.

- Not feeling self-conscious about having this illness.

- Seeking therapy for any co-occurring disorders

- Use healthy coping mechanisms to deal with unpleasant emotions.

- Identify what may cause inappropriate anger or impulsive behavior and devise a safety plan to deal with it.

- Educate yourself about the disease so that you are more informed about its causes and remedies.

- Connect with like-minded individuals to exchange ideas and experiences

It's important to remember that there is no one correct route to recovery from it. The severity of the disease increases throughout adolescence and may progressively improve with age. Many individuals with this personality disorder have more stability in their lives throughout their thirties and forties, when their emotional discomfort decreases as they learn to live meaningful lives.

7.2 Recognizing BPD Triggers

Triggers are specific events or circumstances that cause symptoms to worsen or increase soon after occurring. These occurrences may be exogenous or internal. Its triggers differ from person to person. However, there are several that are common among those suffering from this disorder.

Interpersonal relationships triggers

The most frequent of its triggers are those that arise in a relationship. In many cases, people with a personality disorder have an extremely high sensitivity to abandonment. As a result, they may experience intense fear and violence, impulsivity, self-harm, or even suicidal ideation in a relationship where they feel rejected, criticized, or left. Rejection of any sort, job loss, and the termination of a relationship are all examples of interpersonal life events.

Cognitive Triggers

Thoughts that seem to come out of nowhere may cause severe anxiety and other symptoms of this disorder. Individuals suffering from it due to trauma, such as child abuse, are especially vulnerable to this. A memory, a place, or a picture of a previous experience of trauma or loss may elicit strong emotions in the person who has it.

Not all memories are upsetting; some may be pleasant recollections of times gone by, which can serve as a reminder that things are not as good as they were in the past.

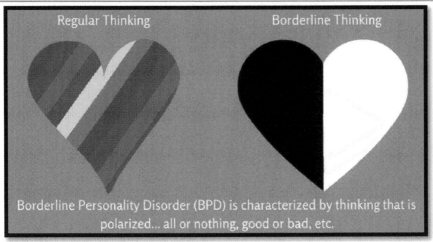

Recognizing the symptoms of a BPD episode

Regular Thinking

Borderline Thinking

Borderline Personality Disorder (BPD) is characterized by thinking that is polarized... all or nothing, good or bad, etc.

To effectively handle its triggers, it is necessary to understand what an episode may feel like. Episodes vary greatly depending on the circumstances and are unique to each person; nevertheless, there are similar themes across the series. An episode of borderline personality disorder is characterized by intense outbursts of rage, as well as episodes of sadness and anxiety.

When they are in the midst of an episode the 85 percent of individuals who present with personality disorder has suicidal thoughts and conduct. Someone suffering from it may become more reclusive and avoidant when experiencing an episode.

It is also typical to have paranoid ideas about everyone being out to get them and disliking them, throughout these periods. Extreme highs, bursts of exhilaration, and pleasant feelings are also possible. Given the extremely impulsive character of individuals suffering from BPD, it is essential to recognize that these emotional highs are also episodes of the illness in their own right. Risky conduct is also a sign of a manic episode of this personality disorder.

7.3 Self-help Tips to Cope with BPD

Three keys to dealing with borderline personality disorder are:
• Calm the raging torrent of emotions.
• Acquire the ability to regulate impulses and tolerating discomfort.
• Improve the ability to interact with others.

Tip One: Calm the raging emotions.

As someone who has this borderline personality disorder, you've undoubtedly spent a lot of time battling your impulses and feelings, making acceptance a difficult concept to grasp. It is important to remember that embracing your feelings does not imply approval or a willingness to endure. To be clear, it simply means that you are no longer engaged in any attempts to resist or avoid your feelings or to conceal or reject them. Allowing oneself to experience these emotions may help to reduce their impact on your well-being.

Make an effort to just experience your emotions without passing judgment or criticism on them. Allow yourself to let go of the past and the future and concentrate only on the present now.

Mindfulness methods are very helpful in this situation.
• Begin by monitoring your feelings as if you were looking in from the outside.
• Keep an eye on them as they arrive and leave (it may help think of them as waves).
• Pay attention to the bodily sensations that occur in conjunction with your emotions.
• Tell yourself that you understand and accept what you are experiencing right now.
• It's important to remind oneself that just because you're experiencing something doesn't imply it's true.

Perform an activity that will excite one or more of your senses.

A sensory engagement is one of the most effective and simple methods to rapidly self-soothe and relax. You will need to explore to determine which sensory-based stimulation is the most effective for you. You'll also need a variety of techniques to suit various emotions. Those that may be helpful while you're furious or irritated are quite different from things that might be helpful when you're numb or sad.

Here are a few suggestions to get you started:

- **Touch:** If you're not feeling well, try rinsing your hands with cold or hot (but not scorching hot) water, holding a piece of ice, or gripping an item or the edge of a piece of furniture as firmly as you possibly can. Taking a hot bath or shower, snuggling beneath your bed covers, or cuddling with a pet may all help you relax if you're experiencing too much emotion.

- **Taste:** To combat the sensation of being empty and numb, try sucking on flavored mints or candies or gently chewing on anything with a strong taste, such as salt or vinegar chips. If you're feeling stressed, try something calming like hot tea or soup to relax.

- **Smell:** Start by lighting a candle, smelling the flowers, experimenting with aromatherapy, spraying your favorite perfume, or cooking something that smells nice in the kitchen. You may discover that strong scents such as citrus, spices, and incense are the ones you react to the most.

- **Sight:** Concentrate on a single picture that catches your attention. The inspiration may be anything in your immediate surroundings (a lovely vista, a gorgeous flower arrangement, a beloved artwork or photo), or it can be something in your mind that you can see.

- **Sound:** Try listening to loud music, using a buzzer, or blowing a whistle when you need to be jolted awake when you're feeling down. To relax, play relaxing music or listen to the calming sounds of nature, such as the wind, birds, or the ocean, to help you decompress.

Take steps to reduce your emotional susceptibility.

When you're exhausted, and under stress, you're more prone to feel unpleasant emotions than when you're not. Taking care of your physical and emotional well-being is thus very essential.

Take good care of yourself by doing the following:
• Reducing stress.
• Exercising regularly.
• Getting enough quality sleep.
• Practicing relaxation methods.
• Avoiding mood-altering substances.
• Eating well-balanced, nutritious food.

Tip Two: Develop the ability to regulate impulses and endure discomfort.

When you are beginning to feel the effects of stress, you may use the soothing methods described above to help you relax. But what should you do if you're feeling overwhelmed by unpleasant emotions and thoughts? Into this situation comes the impulsivity associated with BPD. As a result, you may resort to illegal means of obtaining relief, like engaging in risky sexual behavior and driving recklessly. You may also engage in binge drinking or cutting while under the influence of alcohol or drugs.

Behavioral Control

Making the transition from being out of control of your conduct to controlling your behavior is very important. It's critical to realize that these impulsive actions have a purpose in and of themselves. They are coping strategies used to cope with emotional discomfort. They make you feel better, even if it is just for a short period. The long-term expenses, on the other hand, are very significant. Learning to endure discomfort is the first step toward regaining control of your actions. It is the key to reversing the damaging tendencies of this personality disorder. When you feel the desire to act out, the capacity to endure discomfort will help you put the situation on hold. When faced with unpleasant emotions, you will learn to ride them out while staying in charge of the situation rather than responding with self-destructive habits.

To learn how to ride the wild horse of overpowering emotions, you need to follow a self-guided curriculum, such as the one provided here.

- Come in touch with your emotions.

- Live with emotional intensity.

- Handle unpleasant or frightening sensations.

- Remain calm and focused even when confronted with difficult circumstances.

This enables you to experience the entire spectrum of good emotions such as joy, serenity, and satisfaction, which are otherwise denied to you when you try to avoid bad emotions.

Grounding Exercise

A person cannot think themselves quiet after the fight-or-flight response has been activated. Instead of concentrating on your ideas, pay attention to how you are experiencing in your physical body. The following technique is a simple and fast method to stop impulsivity, calm down, and recover control of one's emotions.

In a matter of minutes, it may make a significant impact on your life.

- Find a peaceful area and sit in a comfortable position.

- Concentrate on the sensations you are having in your body.

- Feel the surface you're sitting on with your whole body.

- Feel the ground under your feet.

- Feel the warmth of your hands on your lap.

- Make a conscious effort to focus on your breathing, taking slow, deep breaths.

- Take a deep breath in gently.

- Take a deep breath and count to three.

- Take a deep breath in and gently exhale counting to three.

- Continue to do so for a few minutes more if necessary.

Distract oneself in the event of an emergency.

It may be beneficial to divert yourself if your efforts to calm down are failing and you are beginning to feel overwhelmed by harmful impulses and thoughts. All you need is anything to divert your attention away from the unpleasant urge for a short period. Anything that attracts your attention may be useful as a distraction, but the most effective distraction is one that is also calming.

In addition to the sensory-based techniques already stated, here are some more things you may want to consider:

- Watch television. Choose something opposed to how you are feeling, such as a comedy if you are depressed or something soothing if you are furious or anxious.

- Make a habit of doing something you love that keeps you occupied. Gardening, decorating, playing an instrument, crocheting, reading a book, playing a computer game, or doing a Sudoku or word puzzle are all examples of activities that fall into this category.

- Put your head down and go to work. Duties and errands may also be used to divert oneself. For example, cleaning your home, performing lawn work, going food purchasing, grooming your pet, or doing the laundry are all good options.

- Commit to being active. Vigorous exercise is a good method to get your adrenaline flowing and blow off some steam simultaneously. If you're feeling anxious, you may want to try some more calming hobbies, such as yoga or taking a stroll around your local area.

- Make a phone call to a buddy. A fast and very efficient method to divert yourself, feel better, and get some perspective is to talk to someone you can trust about your problems.

Tip Three: Improve your Interpersonal abilities.

With a personality disorder, you've likely battled to maintain stable, fulfilling relationships with lovers, coworkers, and friends throughout the years. The reason behind this is that you have a difficult time taking a step back and viewing things from other people's perspectives. You tend to misinterpret the thoughts and emotions of others, to misinterpret how people see you, and to miss how your conduct affects others. It's not that you don't care; it's just that you have a huge blind spot when it comes to the needs of other people.

Understanding your interpersonal blind spot is the first step in overcoming it. As soon as you stop blaming others, you may begin taking measures to enhance your interpersonal connections and social abilities.

Make sure your assumptions are correct.

When you're distracted by stress and negativity, as individuals suffering from it often are, it's easy to misinterpret the intentions of others. If you are aware of this propensity, you should double-check your conclusions. Keep in mind that you are not a mind reader. Instead of rushing to typically negative assumptions, think about what may be driving you in another direction.

Consider the following scenario; your spouse was abrupt with you over the phone, and you are now feeling uncomfortable and fearful that they have lost interest in you because of it. Before you act on your emotions, take a moment to examine the many alternatives. Perhaps your spouse is under a lot of stress at work. Perhaps he is experiencing a difficult day. Perhaps he hasn't had his morning cup of coffee yet. There are a plethora of possible reasons for his actions and inaction.

Inquire as to the person's objectives by asking them to explain them. One of the most straightforward methods to double-check your assumptions is to inquire about the other person about their thoughts or feelings. Check to see whether they meant what they said or did using their words or actions. To avoid seeming accusatory, use a gentler tone when you ask questions.

Put an end to the projections.

Possess you a propensity to take your bad emotions and transfer them onto other people? Is it common for you to lash out at people when you're feeling down on yourself? Is it possible that feedback or constructive criticism is seen as a personal attack? If this is the case, you may be experiencing projection difficulties.

You'll need to learn to apply the brakes to combat projection, just as you did to control your impulsive actions before. Pay attention to your feelings and the actual sensations that you are experiencing in your body. Remember to pay attention to any symptoms of stress, such as a racing heartbeat, tight muscles, sweating, nausea, or light-headedness.

When you're in this frame of mind, you're more likely to go on the offensive and say something you'll later come to regret. Take a few calm, deep breaths and come to a complete stop. Ask yourself the following three questions to help you get started:

- Am I dissatisfied with myself?

- Am I experiencing feelings of embarrassment or fear?

- Do I have concerns about being abandoned?

If you said yes, you should take a break from the discussion.

Inform the other person that you are experiencing emotional turmoil and need some time to reflect before continuing the conversation.

Accept responsibility for your part in the situation.

Finally, it is critical to acknowledge and accept responsibility for your part in your relationships. Consider how your activities may be contributing to the issue. What emotions do your words and actions elicit among your family and friends? Afraid you're about to fall into the trap of viewing the other person as either completely wonderful or completely bad?

Putting yourself in other people's shoes, giving them the benefit of the doubt, and lowering your defensiveness can help you see a change in the quality of your relationships.

7.4 Importance of Diagnosis and Therapy

Keep in mind that you cannot diagnose borderline personality disorder independently; professional assistance is required. Consequently, if you suspect that you or a loved one may have this personality disorder, it is important to get professional assistance.

The significance of selecting the most appropriate therapist

Support and direction from a trained professional may significantly impact the treatment and rehabilitation of borderline personality disorder patients. Psychotherapy may provide a secure environment where you may begin to work through your problems of intimacy and trust while also attempting new coping mechanisms. Although certain treatments are beneficial, it is important to note that following a particular therapeutic strategy is not always essential. Many specialists think that weekly treatment, which includes education on the illness, family support, and social and emotional skills training, may effectively treat the majority of its patients in most instances.

It's important to take the time to locate a therapist with whom you feel comfortable, someone who seems to understand you and who makes you feel welcomed and understood. However, after you have done so, you must commit to treatment. Your therapist may begin by promising to be your savior, only to leave you feeling disappointed and as if they have nothing more to give you in return.

It's important to learn that these fluctuations from glorification to demonization sign of BPD. Make an effort to stick it out with your therapist and allow the connection to develop naturally over time. Also, bear in mind that change is, by its very nature, an unpleasant experience. If you don't ever feel uncomfortable in therapy, likely, you're not making any progress.

Don't depend too much on a pharmaceutical cure.

Even though many individuals with borderline personality disorder use medication, the reality remains that there is very little evidence to suggest that it is beneficial. Furthermore, in the US, the FDA has not authorized any medicines to treat this personality disorder. This does not rule out medication as a treatment option for this disorder, particularly if you suffer from co-occurring disorders such as depression or anxiety. However, medication is not a cure for personality disorder itself.

When it comes to borderline personality disorder, treatment is much more successful. It's simply a matter of giving it some time. However, if you have been diagnosed with depression or any such illness, your doctor may suggest medication as a treatment option.

Some common symptoms that require professional help are:
• You are having panic attacks or experiencing extreme anxiety.
• You are experiencing hallucinations or having strange, paranoid thoughts.

> - You are feeling suicidal or in danger of harming yourself or someone else.

7.5 Providing Support to someone suffering from Borderline Personality Disorder

Do you have a family member or friend who has been diagnosed with a borderline personality disorder? It is impossible to compel someone to get therapy; nevertheless, you may take measures to enhance communication, establish appropriate boundaries, and help your relationship stabilize. People with BPD often have significant problems in their interpersonal interactions, particularly with those closest to them.

It is possible for loved ones to feel powerless, mistreated, and out of balance because of their unpredictable mood swings, violent disorders, chronic abandonment concerns, and other impulsive and illogical actions. Partners and family members frequently describe the emotional roller coaster in the borderline personality disorder relationship as having no end in sight.

The symptoms of this disorder may make you feel stuck in the relationship until you leave or the individual seeks treatment. However, you have more influence than you realize. You may make a difference in your relationship by controlling your emotions, setting clear boundaries, and enhancing communication between you and your partner or spouse.

There is no magic cure for a personality disorder, but with the proper therapy and support, many individuals may improve, and their relationships can become more stable and fulfilling. Patients with the greatest support and stability at home tend to recover more quickly than those with more turbulent and insecure relationships. It doesn't matter whether the person suffering from this disorder is a spouse, parent, offspring, sibling, companion, or other loved one; you can improve both the relationship and your quality of life, even if the person suffering from it isn't ready to recognize the issue or seek therapy.

Learn about this condition

If you or a loved one has this personality disorder, you must realize that he or she is in distress. The damaging and harmful actions are a response to intense emotional anguish and distress. In other words, they aren't interested in you. It's important to remember that when your loved one does or says anything harmful to you, the conduct is usually driven by a desire to alleviate the suffering they are feeling; it's uncommon that the action is intentional.

Learning about a personality disorder may not immediately cure your relationship issues, but it will assist you in better understanding what you're dealing with and dealing with challenges in a more constructive manner.

Recognizing the signs and symptoms

It is not always simple to distinguish between the indications and symptoms of a personality disorder. Unlike other mental illnesses, BPD is seldom diagnosed independently; rather, it is diagnosed in combination with other mental illnesses such as depression, bipolar disorder, anxiety, an eating disorder, or drug addiction. Your family member or loved one who suffers from this disorder may be very sensitive, and even the smallest things may cause them to have severe responses.

When they get angry, borderline individuals are often unable to think clearly or healthily calm themselves. They may say cruel things or behave out in a hazardous or inappropriate manner, for example. Their emotional volatility may create turbulence in their relationships and stress for their families, lovers, and friends as a result.

Many individuals close to BPD are aware that something is wrong with their loved one, but they are unsure of what it is or if there is even a term for it. Receiving a diagnosis of borderline personality disorder may be a source of comfort and optimism for those affected.

Recognizing People affected with BPD

In your partnership:

- Do you ever feel like you have to walk on eggshells around your significant other, monitoring everything you say and do for fear of setting them off?

- Do you frequently keep your thoughts and emotions hidden to prevent arguments and damaged feelings?

- Does your loved one seem to be able to switch between extremes of emotion very instantly? They may be calm one minute, rage the next, and then depressed all at the same time, for example.

- Is it possible that these fast mood swings are unexpected and seem to be irrational?

- Does your significant other tend to see you as either all good or terrible, with no in-between?

- Do you ever feel that you cannot win, as if everything you say or do would be distorted and used to your disadvantage?

- When your loved one's expectations change, do you find yourself unsure of maintaining harmony in your relationship?

- Is it always your responsibility when anything goes wrong?

- Do you ever feel like you're being judged and blamed for things that don't even make any sense to you?

- Is the individual accusing you of doing and saying things that you did not do or say?

- Is it frustrating to feel misunderstood when you're trying to explain or reassure your spouse?

- Do you ever feel like you're being controlled by fear, guilt, or extreme behavior?

- Are they threatening you, flying into violent rages, making theatrical pronouncements, or doing potentially hazardous things when they believe you are unhappy or about to leave them?

If you answered yes to the majority of these questions, your spouse or a member of your family might have a personality disorder.

Take care of yourself first.

To assist someone who has a borderline personality disorder, you must first take care of yourself. The temptation to put out superhuman efforts to satisfy and appease a family member or spouse who has a personality disorder is all too tempting while dealing with this condition. You may find yourself devoting the majority of your attention to the individual suffering from it at the cost of your own emotional needs. Resentment, grief, exhaustion, and even physical disease may result from this kind of living situation.

When you're exhausted and overwhelmed by stress, it's impossible to assist someone else or maintain long-term, meaningful connections with them

. In the case of an emergency in flight, you must first put on your oxygen mask, just as you would in an emergency landing.

- Stay away from the urge to isolate yourself. Maintaining contact with relatives and friends who make you feel good should be a priority.

- You need the assistance of individuals who will listen to you, make you feel cared for, and provide you with reality checks when they are necessary.

- You must permit yourself to live a life apart from your connection with the individual suffering from a borderline personality disorder.

- Participate in a family support group for people with borderline personality disorder. Meeting with people who are experiencing the same thing you are maybe very beneficial. If you cannot locate an in-person support group in your region, you may want to explore becoming a member of an online borderline disorder community.

- Don't forget to take care of your physical well-being. Consuming nutritious foods, engaging in physical activity, and getting enough sleep are all things that may easily go by the wayside when you are involved in a romantic relationship.

- Learn how to deal with stress. The reaction of becoming worried or disturbed in answer to issue response will only serve to exacerbate your chosen one's rage or confusion, as well as your own.

- Using sensory input to train your brain, you may learn to alleviate stress as it occurs while also remaining cool and relaxed when the pressure rises.

Keep in mind the three C's rule.

The damaging conduct of a personality disorder person causes many friends and family members to feel terrible and to blame themselves for their actions. You may wonder what you did to provoke the person's rage, believe that you are somehow deserving of the abuse, or believe that you are to blame for any treatment failures or relapses.

It's essential to remember, though, that you are not accountable for the actions of another individual. The individual suffering with a borderline personality disorder is solely accountable for their acts and behaviors.

The three of them are as follows:
• I was not the one who started it.
• I'm not going to be able to fix it.
• I have no control over it.

Communicating with someone who has BPD

Communication is essential in any relationship, but talking with someone on the verge of being suicidal may be particularly difficult.

People in a close relationship with a borderline adult often compare their conversations with their partner to fighting with a little kid.

People with borderline personality disorder have difficulty interpreting body language and comprehending the nonverbal substance of a discussion. They may express themselves in a harsh, unjust, or illogical manner.

A child's fear of abandonment may lead him or her to overreact to even the smallest perceived insult, and his or her aggressive behavior can manifest itself in spontaneous bouts of rage, verbal abuse, or even physical disturbance. Individuals who suffer from it are that the illness distorts both the signals they receive and the ones they attempt to convey in their daily lives.

One of the most effective methods to assist someone suffering from this disorder is calming down is listening to them, and acknowledging their thoughts and emotions. When you recognize how a borderline person hears you and adapt your communication style with them, you may help defuse the assaults and rages while building a stronger, deeper connection.

Suggestions for Effective Communication

It is critical to understand when it is appropriate to initiate a discussion. The moment to speak with your loved one if they are yelling, verbally abusing you, or making violent threats is not right now.

Much better to postpone the discussion by stating something like:
• Let's speak later when both of us are more relaxed.
• I want to offer you my undivided attention, but it's very difficult for me to do so at this time.
When things are more tranquil:
• Actively listen while being empathetic. Distractions such as the television, computer, or mobile phone should be avoided.
• Make an effort not to interrupt or divert the discussion to your issues or worries.
• Allow yourself to set aside your judgment, refrain from blaming or criticizing, and express your interest in

what is said by periodically nodding or making short vocal remarks.
• It is unnecessary to agree with what the other person is saying to demonstrate listening and empathy.
• Concentrate on the feelings rather than the words. The emotions of the individual suffering from a personality disorder convey much more information than the words they use to express themselves. People who have it need validation and acknowledgment of the anguish they are experiencing.
• Keep your attention on the feeling your loved one is seeking to convey rather than becoming bogged down in trying to reconcile the words used.
• Make an effort to make the individual suffering from it feel heard. It is not appropriate to point out how you believe they are incorrect, attempt to win the debate, or dismiss their emotions, even if what they are saying is completely illogical and unreasonable.
• Make every effort to maintain your composure, especially when the individual with it is behaving out. Avoid being defensive in the face of accusations and criticisms, no matter how unjust you believe the allegations and criticisms are to you. Attempting to defend yourself will make your partner more enraged.

> If you need to give yourself some time and space to calm down, take a step back.

- When your loved one's emotions start to escalate, try to divert their attention. Anything that attracts your loved one's attention may be used as a distraction, but the most effective distraction is one that is also calming to them.

- Discourse on topics other than the illness is encouraged. Make the time to explore and share other hobbies with your loved one since the disease is not the only thing that defines you and your life. Discussions about light topics may help relieve the tension between you and your partner, and they may even inspire your partner to pursue new interests or rekindle old passions.

Don't overlook Self-destructive actions.

If you think a loved one is in imminent danger of suicide, call for help immediately. You shouldn't leave the individual alone. Call the therapist or a suicide prevention hotline.

Setting appropriate limits.

Setting and enforcing appropriate limits or boundaries for a loved one who has a borderline personality disorder is one of the most effective methods to assist them in gaining control over their behavior. Setting boundaries may assist your loved one in better coping with the outside world's expectations, where institutions such as schools, workplaces, and the legal system, among others, all set and enforce tight boundaries on what constitutes acceptable conduct.

In your relationship, establishing boundaries may help replace the chaos and instability of your present arrangement with a much-needed sense of order and provide you with more options for responding when faced with bad conduct. When you'll respect each other's limits, you'll be able to develop a feeling of mutual trust and respect, which are essential components of any lasting relationship. Setting limits, on the other hand, is not a quick cure for a failing relationship. Things may become worse before they get better.

The individual suffering from a personality disorder is terrified of rejection and sensitive to any perceived insult. This implies that if you have never established limits in your relationship before, your partner will likely feel upset when you do so for the first time. The only thing you will accomplish by giving in to your loved one's anger or abuse is that you will reinforce their bad behavior, and the cycle will continue. On the other hand, being strong and sticking to your guns may be very powerful for you and your loved one and can eventually change your relationship.

Learn how to establish and maintain healthy limits.

Talking about limits with your partner should occur when you are both calm and not amid an argument. Decide on what behavior you will and will not accept from the individual and communicate your expectations. To provide an example, you could tell a loved one, "If you can't speak to me without yelling abuse at me, I'm going to walk away."

Do this:
• When imposing boundaries, be calm and reassuring with the individual suffering from a borderline personality disorder. You might say something along the lines of, "I love you, and I want our connection to work, but I can't take the stress you're causing me. I need your assistance in making this adjustment for me."
• Ensure that everyone in the family understands and agrees on the limits and how to enforce the penalties if the boundaries are violated.
• Rather than thinking of establishing limits as a one-time event, see it as a process. Instead of bombarding your loved one with a large list of limits all at once, introduce them one or two at a time, gradually increasing in number.

Don't do this:
• Issue threats and terms that you are unable to follow through on. As is human nature, your loved ones will unavoidably push the boundaries you have established for them. If your loved one will understand that the barrier is worthless if you give in and do not enforce the penalties, they will continue to engage in bad conduct.
• Tolerating abusive conduct is not an option. Any individual should tolerate neither verbal abuse nor physical violence. BPD does not make your loved one's conduct any less harmful to you or other family members just because the behavior results from a disorder.
• Provide support to the individuals suffering from this disorder by shielding them from the repercussions of their behavior. If your loved one refuses to respect your limits and continues to make you feel uncomfortable, you may have no choice but to end the relationship. It does not imply that you do not care about them, but your well-being should always come first.

7.6 Supporting your loved one's Treatment

It is typical for individuals with a personality disorder to delay therapy or reject a problem, even though the condition is extremely durable. However, even if this is the case with your friend or family member, you can still give them support, enhance interaction, and establish limits, all while encouraging them to get professional assistance. The assistance of a competent therapist, even if pharmaceutical choices are restricted, may make a significant difference in your loved one's ability to heal.

Dialectical behavior therapy and Schema-focused therapy are two types of treatments that may assist your loved one in working through their trust and relationship problems as well as exploring new coping strategies. When kids are in treatment, they may learn how to regulate their emotions and comfort themselves healthily.

How to provide support for Treatment

Consider couple's counseling if your loved one refuses to admit that they have a problem with a personality disorder. Instead of focusing on your loved one's illness, the emphasis is on strengthening the connection and encouraging greater communication. Your spouse may be more willing to consent to this and may even consider seeking its treatment in the future if the situation warrants it.

Promote mindfulness and relaxation methods such as yoga, deep breathing, or contemplation to your loved one as a means of dealing with stress and emotions healthily. In addition, sensory-based stimulation may assist them in reducing tension in a time of need. Again, you and your loved one may engage in any of these treatments together, which can help deepen your connection while also encouraging them to explore additional therapy paths if they want to.

Through the development of tolerance for discomfort, your loved one may learn how to take a deep breath and hold it when the desire to act out or behave in an impulsive manner arises.

Setting Objectives for BPD Recovery

Take it easy. It is important to be patient and establish reasonable expectations when assisting your loved ones with their rehabilitation. Change is possible and occurs, but it takes time, just as it does to change any other kind of behavior pattern. Take small steps rather than striving for big, unachievable objectives that will only set you and your loved one up for failure and disappointment in the long run. You and your loved one will have a better chance of success if you reduce your expectations and establish modest, achievable objectives that may be accomplished step by step. Supporting your loved one's rehabilitation may be very difficult and highly gratifying at the same time. You must take care of yourself, but the process may help you develop and improve your connection with your partner.

08

What is Dialectical Behavior Therapy?

This behavioral therapy is a form of cognitive-behavioral therapy that has been adjusted. Its primary objectives are to educate individuals on how to live in the present moment, create healthy coping mechanisms for dealing with stress, control their emotions, and enhance interpersonal connections. The treatment of a personality

disorder was the initial intent of this therapy, but it has now been modified to treat various other mental health problems.

Those who have trouble controlling their emotions or engage in self-destructive conduct may benefit from this treatment, such as eating disorders and substance use disorders. When treating post-traumatic stress disorder, this kind of treatment is sometimes utilized.

8.1 Techniques

This therapy has developed into a research-based psychotherapy technique used to treat a wide range of disorders and illnesses.

The following are examples of situations in which this behavioral therapy is often used:
• Patient-centered group therapy in which patients are taught behavioral skills in a supportive environment.
• Treatment consists of individual treatment with a qualified professional in which a patient's acquired behavioral skills are applied to their life problems.
• When patients contact the therapist between sessions, they may ask for advice on dealing with a tough circumstance they are presently experiencing.

In this therapy, various methods and approaches are used, some of which are detailed below.

Mindfulness

One of the most significant advantages of behavioral therapy is the development of mindfulness abilities. It assists you in concentrating on the current moment or living in the now. You may use this technique to pay attention to what's going on within you, such as your ideas, emotions, sentiments, and desires, as well as utilizing your senses to tune in to what's going on outside of you, such as what you see, listen, smell, and feel in a nonjudgmental manner.

When you are experiencing emotional discomfort, mindfulness skills may assist you in slowing down and concentrating on utilizing appropriate coping mechanisms.

The approach may also assist you in maintaining your composure and avoiding habitual negative thinking patterns and impulsive actions.
• Pay close attention to how you're breathing.
• Take notice of the sensations you get as you inhale and exhale.
• As you breathe, pay attention to how your stomach rises and falls.

Tolerance for Distress

Accepting yourself and your present circumstance is much easier with distress tolerance abilities.

This therapy offers a variety of strategies for dealing with a crisis, including the following:

- Distraction

- Self-soothing

- Increasing the effectiveness of the moment.

- Considering the advantages and disadvantages of not tolerating discomfort.

•

Its methods help you prepare for strong emotions and equip you with the tools you need to deal with them more positively in the long run. When you allow your emotions to follow your body, you may divert yourself from your thoughts.

Effectiveness in Interpersonal Relationships

In a relationship, interpersonal effectiveness helps you become more assertive, for example, by expressing your demands and saying no while still maintaining a pleasant and healthy environment. You will learn to listen and communicate more effectively, cope with difficult individuals, and respect both yourself and others as a result of this experience.

To enhance relationships and good communication, these approaches should be used:

- **Gentle:** Don't attack, threaten, or judge others.

- **Interest:** Demonstrate interest by practicing active listening skills, don't interrupt someone else's speech.

- **Validate:** Recognize and express your understanding of the other person's ideas and emotions.

- **Easy:** Make an effort to maintain a relaxed demeanor, smile often and be light-hearted.

Emotion Regulation

It is possible to regulate your emotions in a more effective way when you are experiencing strong emotions. Identifying, naming, and changing your emotions will be made easier with the abilities you acquire. By learning to identify and manage strong negative emotions (for example, rage), you decrease your risk of experiencing negative emotions and increase your chances of experiencing more good emotional experiences.

Determine how you're feeling and then do the polar opposite of that feeling. If you're feeling down and want to isolate yourself from friends and family, make plans to visit them instead.

8.2 What can Dialectical Behavioral Therapy help with?

Dr. Marsha M. Linehan and her co-workers developed this behavioral therapy in the late 1980s after discovering that cognitive therapy alone did not work as well as expected in patients with a personality disorder. To address the specific requirements of these people, She and her co-workers devised new methods and tailored a treatment plan for them.

While developed with a borderline personality disorder in mind, this therapy may also be an effective treatment for the following conditions:
• Bipolar disorder
• Suicidal self-injury
• Obsessive-compulsive disorder
• Addiction to substances
• Suicidal ideation and behavior
• Major depressive disorder
• Borderline personality disorder
• Hyperactivity-disruptive behavior disorder
• Anxiety disorder with generalized symptoms.
• Eating disorders (such as anorexia, binge eating disorder, and bulimia).

8.3 Advantages of Dialectical Behavioral Therapy

In this behavioral therapy, the patient and the therapist work together to resolve the obvious contradiction among self-acceptance and change to bring about positive changes in the individual enrolled in the program. Part of this process includes providing affirmation, which helps individuals become more inclined to collaborate and less likely to feel pain at the thought of change.

In practice, the therapist confirms that an individual's behaviors make sense within the framework of their own experiences without necessarily agreeing that the actions are the best way to addressing an issue.

However, although each therapeutic environment has its unique structure and objectives, dialectical behavioral therapy features are present in group skills training, individual psychotherapy, and phone coaching.

- **Acceptance and Change:** The methods you'll learn to accept and endure your life circumstances, emotions, and yourself will help you grow as a person. You will also gain knowledge and skills that will enable you to make good changes in your relationships with others and your conduct.

- **Behavioral:** You'll learn how to identify and evaluate problematic or harmful behavior patterns and replace

them with more healthy and productive ones as needed.
• **Social cognition:** You'll work on changing thoughts and feelings that are not productive or beneficial.
• **Collaboration:** You'll communicate efficiently and work collaboratively (therapist, group counselor, psychiatrist).
• **Skill sets:** You will acquire new skills that will help you to be more effective.
• **Encouragement:** You will be encouraged to identify, develop and utilize your positive qualities and traits.

8.4 Effectiveness

This treatment method helps individuals effectively improve their coping abilities, which allows them to build more effective ways to regulate and express intense emotions. The effectiveness of this therapy has also been shown by researchers across various demographics, including age, gender orientation, sexuality, and nationality.

Studies have found this therapy effectively treats a personality disorder and reduces suicide risk in individuals. According to one study, more than 75 percent of people with borderline personality disorder no longer met the diagnostic criteria for the disorder after a year of treatment had been completed. In the case of suicidal behavior, recent research discovered that treatments that included skills training as a therapy component were shown to be more successful in decreasing suicidality than dialectical therapy alone.

The majority of this behavioral therapy research has focused on its efficacy in treating individuals with borderline personality disorder who have suicidal and self-harming thoughts, although the technique may also help treat people with various other mental health problems. For instance, research has shown that this kind of therapy seems to be helpful in the treatment of post-traumatic stress disorder, depression, and fear. Additionally, research indicates this therapy may be beneficial in treating children who suffer from disruptive emotional dysregulation ailment.

Dialectical behavioral therapy necessitates a significant investment of one's time. In addition to regular treatment sessions, individuals are expected to do homework to continue improving their abilities outside of the individual, group, and phone counseling sessions, among other things. People who have trouble keeping up with these tasks regularly may find this a tough task to complete. Exploring traumatic events and emotional suffering occurs at various phases of therapy and may be unpleasant for the patient.

How to Get Started

The most effective way to determine whether this behavioral therapy is right for you is to speak with a trained professional familiar with the method. They will examine your symptoms, treatment history, and therapeutic objectives to determine whether or not dialectical behavioral therapy is a suitable match for your needs. You can also request a referral from your current therapist or another mental wellness expert to a co-worker specializing in this behavior therapy. You may also be able to locate dialectical behavioral therapy therapists that do an online treatment.

8.5 Dialectical Behavior Therapy for Borderline Personality Disorder

Using controlled preclinical studies, the most rigorous form of clinical research, it was the first treatment to be proven to help treat a personality disorder. It is regarded as the gold standard first-line treatment for a personality disorder. While it is no longer the only treatment to have shown efficacy in randomized studies, it has grown a largely empirical basis and is considered one of the best therapies for a personality disorder in terms of recorded survival rates.

Several studies have shown that dialectical therapy helps decrease mental hospitalizations, drug abuse, and suicide attempts. According to Linehan's theory, the core problem in borderline personality disorder is emotional dysregulation, which results from the interaction of biology, including heritable and other biological risk factors with an emotionally unstable childhood environment, for example, when caregivers condemn, marginalize, or react appropriately erratically to the child's experience of anger.

The primary goal of this therapy is to assist the client in learning and using strategies that will reduce emotion dysregulation and inappropriate efforts to deal with intense emotions. It is cognitive-behavioral therapy.

What to Expect from this Therapy?

However, there are certain exceptions to this rule. Typically, it consists of a mix of group skills development, personal psychotherapy, and phone counseling. Patients undergoing this therapy are asked to track their symptoms and use newly acquired skills daily, and their progress is tracked throughout therapy. A total of four major kinds of skills training are addressed in this therapy skills training sessions. These are:

1. Techniques for Mindfulness Meditation

Mindfulness contemplation techniques are centered on being completely in the present. To develop these skills, students must first learn to observe, describe and take part in all experiences - including but not limited to; thoughts, feelings, and events occurring in the outside world. Students must also learn to participate in all experiences without judging them as good or bad.

These are regarded as basic abilities that are required to apply other behavioral therapy skills effectively. For example, individuals with a borderline disorder may find themselves struggling with feelings during a disagreement and may subsequently act out on those sentiments without contemplating the repercussions. Developing mindfulness skills can assist individuals in learning how to perceive and control their emotions, allowing them to take a step back and react more adequately.

2. Interpersonal Effectiveness Skills

When it comes to relationships, the emphasis of this skill module is on learning to assert your needs while also managing conflict effectively.

3. Ability to Handle Difficult Situations

The anxiety tolerance skills module encourages the development of strategies for accepting and tolerating discomfort without resorting to actions that may exacerbate the distress in the long term, such as self-harm or substance abuse. When confronted with intense emotion, a person who has this disorder may engage in impulsive or potentially dangerous actions in an attempt to escape what they perceive to be an unbearable sensation.

People may engage in hazardous behaviors such as substance abuse, offensive, excessive alcohol misuse, and other potentially dangerous activities to feel better for a short period. The issue is that this kind of action exacerbates the situation in the long run. People can develop distress tolerance skills, which allow them to better cope with negative emotions and respond in more adaptive ways.

4. Emotional Self-Control and Regulation

In this lesson, patients learn to recognize and regulate emotional responses. To react effectively and accomplish individual objectives, it is necessary to regulate emotions. This includes boosting or decreasing emotions. Developing these emotional skills enables individuals with a personality disorder to understand their feelings better and discover methods to regulate and express them in a healthy and non-destructive manner. For example, knowing how to tolerate feelings, alter actions to change a situation, or find other methods to cope with emotion without lashing out are all skills that may be developed.

It is not a solution for borderline personality disorder, although it may be extremely helpful for decreasing or managing symptoms of the disease. According to one research, after a year of dialectical behavior therapy, 77% of individuals no longer fulfilled the criteria for a personality disorder. Alternatively, you may contact your therapist, doctor, or other mental health experts to recommend someone who expertise in this therapy.

8.6 The Difference Between Dialectical Behavior Therapy and Didactic Therapy

Didactic therapy is a kind of group treatment that is most often used to teach people with drug use disorders the facts and educate themselves, while dialectical behavioral therapy is most commonly used to treat a personality disorder. Dialectical therapy for a personality disorder is a type of cognitive therapy that has been scientifically proven to reduce the distressing symptoms of this disorder, including self-harm and suicide attempts. Dialectical therapists receive extensive training in behavior therapy for a personality disorder.

Dialectical therapy focuses on teaching behavioral skills such as controlling emotions, being present in the moment, enduring distress, and managing relationships with other people, among other things. Individual and group therapy sessions and phone coaching sessions are all used to implement this therapy technique. Therapists that specialize in dialectical therapy are difficult to find. Treatment programs may be found by searching for them by continent, nation, and then state or province, among other criteria.

If none of these databases prove to be of use, you may consider contacting psychology or psychiatry departments at nearby universities, institutes, or medical facilities. Because dialectical therapy is an evidence-based method of treatment, ongoing education departments may include professionals who have received its training. As an additional option, you might try searching for the government agency responsible for meeting the mental health needs of the people in your region.

This may be the department of social services, mental health, or a comparable organization in your area. These organizations may be aware of their therapists in your region and may be able to assist you in obtaining a referral based on your need. It's a good idea to discuss your intention to explore this therapy with your primary care physician or psychiatrist before beginning the treatment. Your doctor may send you to a specialist and assist you in determining if this is the most appropriate treatment strategy for you.

8.7 Cognitive Behavioral Therapy vs. Dialectical Behavior Therapy for BPD

Are these forms of therapy distinct from one another, or are they just variants on one another? Now, let's take a deeper look at these different kinds of behavioral treatments and how they are linked to one another.

Cognitive Behavioral Therapy

It is a kind of therapy in which the patient uses his or her thoughts to solve problems. This therapy, often known as CBT, attempts to reorganize and alter the way a person thinks and acts to improve their overall well-being. The quality of the connection between the person and their therapist significantly impacts whether or not this treatment is helpful. The willingness of the person to make a change is also an important consideration.

Cognitive restructuring and behavioral changes, such as decreasing self-defeating habits and learning how to react to situations in a healthy, adaptive way, are examples of methods employed by a behavioral therapist. In cognitive restructuring, a patient is trained to recognize negative reactive thoughts and to change those negative reactive ideas.

Dialectical Behavioral Therapy

It is a kind of behavioral therapy specifically designed to treat borderline personality disorder. This method is dialectical because it includes two opposing concepts; treating this disorder's symptoms requires both acceptance and change and improvement. In particular, it emphasizes the development of skills such as mindfulness, being in the present now, mood management, enduring pain, and successfully managing interpersonal interactions.

In Studies it's the only effective therapy for borderline personality disorder. It comprises four components that the person and therapist typically work on together over a year or more.

These components are:
- **The individual treatment:** uses cognitive restructuring and exposure methods to help patients alter their behavior and enhance overall well-being.
- **Group therapy**: teaches patients how to react effectively to tough issues or circumstances via the application of skills training.
- **Telephone conversations:** that focus on applying newly acquired skills to everyday life outside of treatment.
- **Weekly consultation sessions among the participants in this therapy:** provide support for the therapists and an opportunity to check that they are following the dialectical treatment paradigm.

This therapy also assists individuals with borderline personality disorder in developing skills such as the ability to endure discomfort, regulate emotions, and engage in successful interpersonal interaction. People who use this therapy are more likely to learn how to cope with intense emotions and develop new methods of dealing with strong feelings without reverting to harmful coping strategies, which is a primary emphasis of the treatment. Developing generalized anxiety, for example, is concerned with assisting individuals in recognizing and accepting unpleasant emotions without resorting to destructive actions such as self-harming.

8.8 How to Choose the Best Treatment for you?

You should consult with your doctor about locating the most appropriate therapist and treatment model to feel better and enhance your overall quality of life. Dialectical therapy is essentially a modified type of cognitive therapy that uses conventional cognitive-behavioral methods while additionally emphasizing the development of other skills such as mindfulness, acceptance, and the ability to tolerate discomfort.

The good news is that dialectical therapy is much more successful than traditional psychotherapy in treating personality disorders. This therapy is suggested as a first-line treatment for borderline personality disorder, and it has been proven to decrease the requirement for medical care and medicines by as much as 90 percent in certain instances. Interestingly, some behavioral therapists integrate aspects of the dialectical therapy paradigm into their therapy sessions. In addition, various types of cognitive therapy have emerged that include aspects of this therapy. For example, mindfulness-based cognitive treatment, which combines conventional cognitive-behavioral methods with mindfulness to treat depression, is becoming very popular.

09

Transference-Focused Therapy and Schema-Focused Therapy

In treating this personality disorder, transference-focused therapy is a kind of therapy that focuses on changing the way  you interact with other people in the world via your therapeutic relationship with your therapist. This may assist you in identifying troubling thoughts, developing better habits, and improving social relationships.

9.1 What is Transference-Focused Therapy and How does it Work?

Transference is a theoretical process in which emotions are transmitted from one person to another via the exchange of information. When it comes to dynamic psychotherapies, this one is a critical topic to understand. According to the theory behind these treatments, the therapist will read your thoughts and emotions about significant individuals in your life, such as your parents or siblings.

Through transference, it is hoped that the therapist will observe your interactions with other people and utilize this knowledge to assist you in developing more healthy connections. Therapists specializing in this focused treatment for borderline personality disorders think that the primary etiology of this disorder is linked to dysfunctional connections in childhood that continue to affect teenage and adult relationships.

According to this idea, our sense of self and mental representations of others are formed via our interactions with our caregivers throughout early infancy. If anything goes wrong during this process, we may have trouble developing a strong sense of self or experiencing difficulties in our relationships with other people.

A growing number of research suggests that early maltreatment or the loss of primary caregivers during childhood increases the risk of developing borderline personality disorder and because the symptoms of it include significant difficulties in interpersonal relationships and an unstable sense of one's own identity, some experts have proposed that it should be treated by fostering healthier relationships through the use of transference.

9.2 Transference-Focused Therapy Techniques

People who are participating in this therapy meet with their psychotherapist twice a week. During these appointments, the therapist will use methods from the field of object relations which has as its key component the emphasis placed on the significance of social contact in helping individuals alter their maladaptive habits.

These methods may include the following:
• Establishing a relationship of trust between the therapist and the patient.
• Establishing limits that are unique to the individual's symptoms.
• The study of behavior patterns, emotions, and one's sense of self, and how these factors affect one's capacity to deal with adversity.
• Increased awareness of harmful or hazardous actions.
• Developing the ability to change emotional states and enhance relationships to alleviate symptoms.

Transference-Focused Therapy for Other Conditions

Even though transference psychotherapy was created to treat individuals with a personality disorder, it may be useful for various other problems and conditions:

- Improving one's ability to regulate their emotions.

- Decreased signs and symptoms of anxiety and sadness.

- Reducing the likelihood of self-harm and suicidal thoughts.

- Increasing the effectiveness of social interactions and partnerships.

- Lowering the severity of symptoms such as rage, impulsivity, and irritability.

9.3 Advantages of Transference-Focused Therapy

More study is required to establish how effective this method is in comparison to other types of therapy.

However, some potential advantages include the following:

- Supporting individuals in identifying and eliminating internalized beliefs that lead to harmful behaviors.

- Enabling individuals to get a greater understanding of how their ideas influence many aspects of their lives.

- Facilitating the integration of many aspects of a person's ideas and beliefs to foster a more coherent sense of self

Effectiveness of Transference-Focused Therapy

The use of this treatment for personality disorder seems to be supported by preliminary studies. It was discovered in 2007, this therapy was equivalent to dialectical behavior therapy in reducing some symptoms of borderline personality disorder such as suicidal thoughts and was superior to dialectical therapy in reducing other symptoms, such as impulsive behaviors or anger. This study was one of the most rigorous forms of research available at the time.

This focused psychotherapy was more successful than treatment by experienced community psychotherapists in decreasing personality disorder symptoms, increasing psychosocial functioning, and enhancing personality structure in a subsequent randomized controlled research. The findings also seemed to be more successful in reducing suicidal ideation and the need for in-patient therapy.

9.4 TFP Related Questions and Concerns

It is essential to highlight that, even though current research indicates that extended treatment with this therapy may be effective, some experts still regard this kind of therapy as rather controversial. More research is required to understand further how long this therapy's effects may continue and if it may be a better option than other treatment methods. However, it is important to note that the randomized controlled trial had a significant limitation: patients in this therapy group received significantly more individual psychotherapy than those in the dialectical therapy condition, even though this is promising preliminary evidence of the treatment's effectiveness.

Transference treatment may be as effective as, if not more effective than, dialectical therapy in decreasing symptoms of personality disorders; however, it is also conceivable that the gains were due to the patients getting more therapy. More study is required to determine whether or not this therapy is effective.

How to Get Started?

This treatment for borderline personality disorder focuses on the relationship between you and your therapist. The therapist will seldom offer you advice or give you specific instructions on what to do. Instead, the therapist will most likely ask you many questions and guide you through the process of exploring your responses throughout sessions. Instead of focusing on the past, the present is the focal point of attention. You will likely spend more time talking about how you connect to your therapist than you will spend time talking about how you relate to others.

In this kind of treatment, it is also common for the therapist to maintain objectivity by avoiding offering their viewpoint and being accessible outside of the therapy session, unless in emergencies. Consider discussing with your therapist whether or not this therapy may be a good fit for your situation. They will go through the advantages and disadvantages of this kind of treatment with you and may suggest based on your specific condition and circumstances.

What can Transference-Focused Therapy Help with?

The majority of the study on this therapy has looked at how it affects people who have been diagnosed with a borderline personality disorder.

- Increased social contact.

- Decreased suicidal ideation.

- It has been shown to effectively reduce this disorder's symptoms: impulsivity, annoyance, rage, and self-harm.

- It has also been shown to improve emotional control.

According to the researchers, some early studies also support this therapy for other mental health concerns such as narcissism. Because narcissism and borderline personality disorder may share certain characteristics linked to social interactions, it may be useful for detecting comparable patterns in people who have a narcissistic personality disorder.

9.5 What is the Method by which TFP works?

This therapy employs an object relations-based therapy method delivered twice weekly to change and enhance entrenched behavioral patterns that may be harmful or unhealthy. Object relations theory views that people are driven more by social contact and connections with other humans than by sex or hostility with other humans. By approaching behaviors from the perspective that all individuals genuinely desire to better their relationships with others, therapists can concentrate on how someone may achieve permanent change rather than on the apparent pathologies of the individual.

Two core principles govern the practice of transference-focused therapy:
• Identifying symptoms as internal causes and emotional states rather than external manifestations that can be seen with the naked eye.
• Grow and refine their knowledge of the client's symptoms or problematic behaviors.

When someone is in therapy, it encourages them to accept responsibility for their actions and behaviors, based on the understanding that while a person's personality disorder diagnosis may be permanent, how they cope with its symptoms and interacts with others can change and improve throughout therapy. Whenever a person notices or is presented in real-time changes in their emotional state or interaction approach, they are given the option to choose more beneficial choices.

It is assumed that these are the only or main problems for which an individual seeks treatment since it is a highly specialized approach intended to address difficulties linked to personality and interpersonal interactions. It may not be the best first step in psychotherapy for someone who is also dealing with mental health issues such as drug or alcohol abuse, eating disorders, or severe suicidal ideation in addition to other issues. Those who have these illnesses or concerns may want to consider complementary therapy before starting it or in conjunction with this treatment.

What happens in a TFP Session?

The therapist will work with the client to obtain informed consent in the earliest phases when starting this treatment. Because it is a unique therapeutic technique that usually relies on a more active approach from the psychotherapist than other kinds of talk therapy, it is essential that a person starting it feels completely comfortable with their therapist before moving further.

Treatment is divided into two stages, which may sometimes overlap or continue to weave together throughout a treatment:
• Establishing trust, a treatment framework that will guide future sessions, and boundaries unique to a person's particular destructive habits are important components of the therapy process.
• The second step involves exploring and reviewing the individual's cognition, sense of identity, emotions, and recurrent behavioral patterns. Moments of emotional instability, aggressiveness, defensiveness, or other responses may arise when the person and the therapist work through identifying problems and behavioral patterns.

Each of these instances provides the psychotherapist with a chance to bring attention to the emotional shift or change in behavior. Coming to grips with one's own detrimental thinking patterns or emotional responses may be a very raw and unpleasant process; nevertheless, most study findings linked to this treatment indicate that this kind of therapy is effective.

According to the findings, clinical studies are most successful when used consistently for at least one year to develop a trusting therapeutic connection and provide enough time to focus on key goals stated early in treatment.

9.6 Risks and Limitations

The majority of studies found that extended this therapy was linked with high success rates. Those trials that produced dubious findings did not prove that it was unsuccessful; rather, they raised additional concerns about how long the effects would persist and if this therapy was a superior treatment option to another treatment, such as schema-focused therapy.

Given that transpersonal psychotherapy seems reserved for people with personality disorders, it is unclear if this modality would succeed in groups with a borderline diagnosis. The effectiveness of this treatment for persons with borderline personality disorder and those with other mental health problems requires further study.

9.7 What is Schema-Focused Therapy?

This treatment is a kind of psychotherapy that focuses on recognizing and altering particular problematic thinking patterns when it comes to borderline personality disorder. However, in addition to certain aspects that are typical components of cognitive-behavioral therapy, the treatment also incorporates elements from other kinds of psychotherapy, including psychodynamic therapy.

9.8 How does Schema Therapy Work?

Individuals can grow up with deficits in their abilities to meet their emotional needs, their basic needs for affection and guidance, and love, shelter and safety, if they do not receive the emotional support, they require as children. This can occur

both independently and through healthy relationships with each other.

A fundamental tenet of this therapy is that early maladaptive schemas are formed due to these traumatic childhood events. Individuals who have maladaptive schemas, which can be described as ways in which they interpret life situations and the actions of others, can later experience life disruptions, including making unhealthy choices, forming toxic relationships, lacking fully developed social skills, engaging in destructive behavior patterns, having poor knowledge of the issues, and experiencing feelings of hopelessness or self-doubt, among other things.

This therapy is centered on the identification and modification of dysfunctional schemas. Through this therapy, individuals may begin to develop emotions of self-worth and sufficiency by identifying the sources of their unmet emotional needs and learning how to establish supportive connections. The following therapeutic methods may be used throughout this process:

Imagery

Therapy participants use imagery to examine unpleasant childhood experiences to understand the formation of maladaptive schemas better. Initially, individuals are encouraged to picture the views, sounds, and other sensations associated with these memories. They are then instructed to engage in imaginative conversation with the caregivers associated with these memories to fulfill their needs. Following this process, people are typically better able to recognize present circumstances that evoke similar feelings, and they may be more effective in healthily meeting their needs in the future.

Diaries

Individuals seeking schema therapy are often instructed to maintain a journal or record any events that trigger early maladaptive schemas. Individuals may learn to recognize the thought patterns that are linked with these schemas while in therapy. When these thought patterns arise between sessions, the journal allows people to write about the events, emotions, and actions that are connected with them. In the session, these diaries are examined and may be useful in identifying the best techniques for developing new ways of fulfilling emotional needs and the circumstances in which these approaches may be used most effectively.

Flashcards

In this therapy, therapists work with clients to help them construct messages intended for the caregivers who failed to fulfill their emotional needs during their formative years. These communications can take the shape of simple remarks, notes, or even elaborate poetry. In most cases, the individual undergoing therapy will review the cards in between sessions.

This periodic review is designed to assist individuals in learning how to communicate their emotional needs to significant others in their adult life healthily and successfully.

Chairwork

It is an element of therapy that aims to assist people receiving treatment in identifying variances in their emotions and personalities. The individual in treatment goes between two seats, expressing various emotions and parts of their personality in each chair as they move between them. It may also assist someone undergoing treatment in seeing themselves having conversations with family members, friends, or other important people. If a person is engaged in this kind of chair work, they may make comments about their emotional needs while seated in one chair and then go to another chair to play the part of someone who may fulfill those needs. Imagination work is often carried out in combination with chair work.

9.9 Childhood Needs and Schemas Therapy

Essentially, the theory underlying this focused therapy asserts that if we do not receive adequate attention to our basic childhood needs, such as those for safety, acceptance, and love, we will develop unhealthy ways of interpreting and interacting with the world, which is referred to as maladaptive early schemas. They are broad and widespread patterns of thought and behavior that many people use. They are more than simply beliefs; they are deeply ingrained patterns intimately associated with our sense of ourselves and our perspective on the universe.

It is hypothesized by this theory that events occurring in our present lives stimulate the activation of schemas when they are similar to events that occurred in our past that were associated with the development of schema therapy. Developing unhealthy schemas due to unpleasant events in our childhood will lead to us responding in unhealthily harmful ways to a new circumstance if we have previously established unhealthy schemas.

It is important to note that not having your basic emotional needs fulfilled as a kid is one of the most significant elements in forming schemas.

These basic requirements include:
• A feeling of safety and being firmly connected to people.
• A strong feeling of one's own identity and autonomy.
• The ability to explain yourself and ask for what you need from others without being judged.

- The capacity to engage in playful and spontaneous behavior.

- Limits and boundaries that are safe and age-appropriate.

As a bonus, these kinds of unpleasant events may contribute to the formation of schemas.

These are some examples:

- **Unfulfilled needs.** You may experience this if you do not get love from caretakers or have your other basic emotional needs fulfilled.

- **Traumatization or victimization**. This depicts a scenario in which you were subjected to abuse, trauma, or other forms of suffering.

- **Overindulgence or a failure to set boundaries.** You may have been subjected to an excessive amount of protection or involvement by your parents during this period. It's possible that they didn't establish appropriate limits for you.

- **Identification and internalization selective**. You may have absorbed some of your parents' attitudes or actions.

Some of these may evolve into schemas, while others may develop into modes, also known as coping mechanisms.

According to this theory, many personality disorder symptoms are triggered by adverse childhood events, such as abuse or early separation from caregivers, resulting in maladaptive schemas.

Examples

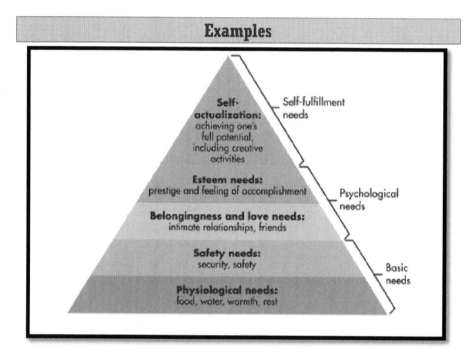

Understanding how schema therapy works requires looking at some of the problematic early schemas that individuals may have and the problems that these may create in the future.

The following are a few instances of schemas:

- The fear of being abandoned: it may drive people who think they are inherently unlovable to destroy their relationships out of a sense of deficiency or shame.

- Avoidance: a behavior in which individuals attempt to avoid any circumstance that causes them to feel dread or vulnerability.

- Overcompensation: doing in actions that directly contradict the belief and are frequently carried out to an excessive degree.

- People who believe they cannot be happy or successful unless they support other people, usually family members, may become excessively reliant on their family members.

- They may be lacking in terms of a feeling of direction, autonomy, and uniqueness.

According to the theories of schema therapy, there are three main coping strategies that individuals use to cope with these beliefs.

9.10 What exactly are the Various Schemas?

Schemas are most often formed in infancy and are notoriously difficult to alter once established. However, if left unchecked, schemas may result in harmful habits often reinforced via unhealthful social interactions. An established schema may subconsciously affect your ideas and behaviors to avoid emotional discomfort.

The coping mechanisms that schemas generate are often unhealthy or dangerous, even though they seem to be beneficial.

The majority of individuals have more than one schema in their heads. However, experts have discovered eighteen different schemas, which are all classified into one of five groups or domains:

1. **Separation and rejection**: it contain schemas that make establish and maintain good friendships and partnerships.

2. **Poor autonomy and performance**: difficulties in establish a strong sense of self and operate in the world as an adult.

3. **Impaired limits:** contains schemas that interfere with one's capacity to maintain self-control and respect boundaries and limitations.

4. **Other directedness**: have schemas that encourage you to put the needs of others ahead of your interests.

5. **Over vigilance and inhibition**: comprises schemas that emphasize avoiding failure or errors by being attentive, following rules and disobeying wants or emotional impulses.

9.11 What kinds of Coping Mechanisms do Schemas engender?

Coping styles are used in schema therapy to describe how you respond to schemas presented to you. These may take the form of ideas, emotions, or behavioral patterns. As a consequence of a particular schema, they evolve to avoid the unpleasant and overpowering feelings associated with it. Coping methods may be beneficial in childhood since they serve as a way of ensuring one's survival. However, in maturity, they may serve to reinforce preconceived notions.

There are no hard and fast rules regarding which schemas are associated with different coping strategies. Depending on your general disposition or even the coping methods you acquired from your parents, your coping style may be determined. They also differ from one individual to the next. Two individuals responding to the same schema with the same style in quite different ways.

Your coping technique may also evolve with time, even though you are still dealing with the same schema in the long run. The following are some primary coping strategies, which are roughly associated with the fight-or-flight or freeze response:

Surrender

This entails agreeing to a paradigm and giving in to its demands. As a consequence, it often leads to behavior that reinforces or maintains the schema pattern. For example, suppose you succumb to a schema that developed due to emotional neglect as a kid. In that case, you may eventually find yourself in a relationship where you are subjected to emotional neglect yourself.

Avoidance

It leads avoid engaging in activities or circumstances that might potentially set your disease off or make you feel vulnerable. You may become more susceptible to drug abuse, hazardous or obsessive behavior, and other activities that serve as a diversion.

Overcompensation

This entails making an effort to defeat a schema by behaving in full contradiction to it. Although this may seem to be a good reaction to a schema, overcompensation is usually taken to an extreme. It often results in acts or behaviors that are seen as aggressive, demanding, insensitive, or excessive in some manner. This may have a negative impact on your interpersonal connections.

What are Schema Modes, and how do they Work?

In this therapy, a mode is a transitory state of mind that encompasses both your current emotional state and your approach to coping with that state of mind. As a result of the mix of active schemas and coping methods, your mode may be beneficial or detrimental. These modes assist therapists in grouping schemas together to treat them as a unified state of mind rather than as a collection of separate characteristics.

Schema modes may be classified into four types, which are as follows:

- **Kid modes**: defined by emotions and actions that are similar to those of a child.

- **Dysfunctional coping mechanisms**: used to alleviate emotional pain, but they serve to reinforce the schema.

- **Dysfunctional parent modes:** internalizations of critical, demanding, or harsh parental voices.

- **Healthy adult mode:** reflects your best, most functional version of yourself. This mode may aid in the regulation of the other modes by establishing boundaries and counteracting the impacts of the other modes on the system.

9.12 Goals of Schema Therapy

The first objectives of this focused treatment for a borderline personality disorder are to identify the patient's relevant schemas and establish a connection between these and previous events and present symptoms. Following this initial work, the therapist and patient will collaborate to develop strategies for processing emotions associated with the schemas, changing unhealthy coping patterns that are the consequence of maladaptive and modifying the schemas themselves. When dealing with anger, the therapist and client may utilize many techniques like breaking harmful behavior habits and altering unhelpful thought patterns to assist the client express.

In schema therapy, you and your therapist will work together to:
• Recognize and resolve coping methods that are interfering with the satisfaction of emotional needs.
• Shift emotional and behavioral habits that are a consequence of schema formation.
• Learn how to meet your most basic emotional demands in a healthy and adaptable manner.
• Find out how to deal with irritation and discomfort healthily.

All of this will aid you in developing a strong and healthy adult mode. When you have a well-developed healthy adult mode, it may aid in the healing and regulation of other modes, as well as preventing you from being overwhelmed by their effects.

Research Support

While there has not yet been extensive research into schema-focused therapy, one study has been published to date suggests that patients randomly assigned to receive this focused therapy had significantly greater reductions in personality disorder symptoms than those randomly assigned to receive psychodynamic therapy. While there is early evidence of the efficacy of this therapy, it indicates that this approach has potential in the treatment of borderline personality disorder. A review of numerous research papers on psychological treatment for borderline personality disorder similarly concluded that it seems helpful, although the authors also stated that further research is required.

Finding a competent practitioner with previous experience with this therapy may be difficult, but tools are available to assist in this endeavor. It is possible to begin by searching for behavioral therapists in your region who are trained in this approach. Because it employs many cognitive therapy methods, these therapists may be familiar with both approaches.

9.13 Uses of Schema Therapy

It was discovered that not only were some mental health concerns particularly difficult to treat, but that aspects of these situations continued to create issues for some people even after receiving generally effective treatment. This therapy is recommended to treat mental health problems affecting individuals across many periods and aspects of life more successfully.

Studies on this therapy have shown that this kind of treatment is frequently helpful in treating the following issues:
• Eating disorders
• Criminal behavior
• Anxiety Disorders
• Abuse of drugs and alcohol
• Posttraumatic stress disorder
• Depression that lasts a long time
• Problems in interpersonal relationships

Schema therapy has been proven to be especially successful in treating personality disorders, and research has shown that people enrolled in this therapy leave the program at a lower rate than those enrolled in other kinds of therapy.

Because people with narcissism personalities are not often seeking treatment, more study may be required to completely establish this therapy as a viable treatment option for it.

9.14 Risks and Limitations

When it comes to psychological intervention, schema therapy is a relatively young field of study, and research into this treatment method is still in its early stages. A recent assessment of studies on schema therapy discovered preliminary indications of its efficacy and highlighted the need for a complete research foundation on positive results and cost-efficiency of the treatment.

One of the most common concerns about this therapy is the expense and time to complete the treatment. Given that it effectively treats chronic issues, treatment typically takes longer and costs more than other evidence-based treatments, which is understandable given their effectiveness. However, it may be less costly than the expenses associated with chronic mental health problems that are not effectively addressed in the long run. This is because chronic mental illnesses are frequently quite expensive to healthcare systems if left unchecked.

10

Mentalization-based Treatment for Borderline Personality Disorder

It is a complicated and severe mental illness defined by a persistent pattern of problems with emotion management, anger control and instability in interpersonal relationships and  self-image. Given its association with suicide tries and injury, it is considered a significant public health issue.

Patients with a personality disorder report recurrent suicidal behavior in 80 percent of cases, with suicide rates considered to be as high as 15 percent. It is a disease that affects people worldwide. The high incidence of this disorder and the higher suicide rate among patients with personality disorder provides an irrefutable case for the development of effective treatments and the availability of effective treatments to a larger number of people.

A variety of therapies for this personality disorder have been proven to be somewhat successful in random controlled investigations, but it is still of great concern because the majority of these treatments need significant training, which makes them inaccessible to the majority of patients.

To address this, the mentalization-based therapy model was created. Compared to overall mental health training, it necessitates only a small amount of additional training, and it has been successfully performed in analysis by community mental wellness experts, most notably nurses, who received only rudimentary training and were subjected to modest levels of administration.

10.1 What is Mentalization-based Treatment and how does it Work?

It was initially used in a wider sense in 1989 and has since been refined to understand various mental illnesses. When we make meaning of ourselves, completely and overtly, in terms of discriminatory experiences and mental methods, we are said to be mentalizing, or better said to be better mentalizing. It is a fundamentally social construct because we are acutely aware of people's mental states with whom we are actually or psychologically interacting. Because of the broad scope of this concept, most psychic illnesses will inevitably have some difficulty with mentalization at some point.

We may think of most psychic disorders as being caused by the mind misunderstanding its perception of itself, which results in a disease of mentalization in the end. The most important question is whether the disorder is central to the illness and, if a center is heuristically legitimate, whether it offers a useful domain for curative intervention in the first place.

This approach is also being used to treat a variety of other disorders:
• Post-traumatic stress disorder
• Eating disorders
• Depression

It is used in various settings, including inpatient, partial hospitalization, outpatient departments, and various patient populations, including adolescents, families, and drug abusers. The method is most clearly established as a therapy for personality disorder.

Mentalizing refers to our capacity to pay attention to mental states in ourselves and others as we try to comprehend our behaviors and those of others based on deliberate mental states. It is a skill that can be developed through time. If we are successful in our mentalization, we will be able to comprehend what is going on in our minds as well as the minds of others, and we will be able to recognize how this is affecting our own emotions, thoughts, and actions, as well as the emotions, thoughts, and actions of others. Having a better knowledge of our views and the perspectives of others allows us to have more effective interactions and common connections. Individuals suffering from certain mental health problems, such as personality disorders, may not mentally process information.

Consequently, misconceptions about emotions, ideas, and behaviors may arise, resulting in disintegrating friendly interactions and interpersonal relationships. People must learn how to mentalize to enhance their mental health and social functioning effectively. This therapy is based on teaching people to imagine as a therapeutic intervention mentally. Evidence-based therapy for personality disorder has been proven to be extremely successful, and as a consequence, it has received widespread national and worldwide attention. A weak mentalizing ability that is susceptible to social and interpersonal interaction is a characteristic of borderline disorder.

When it comes to therapeutic effectiveness, it is essential that the therapy either focuses on mentalization therapy itself or, at the absolute least, stimulates its growth as an epiphenomenon. Most therapists were aware of the failure of grown-up cerebral processing in borderline circumstances, but none had recognized the main problem as a lack of mentalizing that had occurred during early development.

A straightforward and fundamental point we made was that the ability to represent oneself and others as reasoning, understanding, wanting or desiring did not emerge at age five as a result of maturation but preferably as a developmental accomplishment that was thoroughly rooted like early object relationships. The predictability of its vulnerability to dissolution under tension in borderline conditions was considered an appropriate focus for psychodynamically turned into emotional intervention, even though concerns had been expressed for decades about using psychodynamic therapy in treating personality disorder.

10.2 Development of Mentalization Treatment

Although it has its roots in accessory theory and its refinement by modern developmental psychologists, the mentalizing theory also considers constitutional vulnerabilities. According to some research, borderline individuals may have a history of disordered attachment, resulting in difficulties with emotion regulation, attention, and self-control. The inability to acquire a strong mentalizing capability, according to our hypothesis, is the cause of these difficulties. Our ability to comprehend the mental states of others is crucially dependent on whether or not we were properly understood as babies by loving, attentive, non-threatening adults. The most common source of disruption in mentalizing is psychological trauma experienced early or late in childhood, which impairs the ability to think about one's mental states and provide narrative descriptions of one's previous interpersonal interactions.

Based on growing evidence from developmental psychopathology, this theory of personality disorder first suggests that individuals are constitutionally vulnerable and exposed to psychological trauma; second, that both of these factors can impair the improvement of cognitive functions necessary for it through negligence in early relations, particularly where the contingency is a concern.

Leftovers of attachment issues from infancy may manifest themselves in adulthood, given the well-documented continuity of attachment patterns through time. Suppose a direct link can be established between a personality disorder diagnosis and a particular attachment type. In that case, there is no question that it is significantly linked with an insecure attachment. There is evidence that early attachment insecurity is a rather persistent feature of its patients, especially when associated with later negative life events, e.g., divorce.

10.3 Clinical Treatment Based on Mentalization

The focus of treatment for a personality disorder should be on stabilizing the sense of self and assisting the patient in maintaining an optimal level of arousal in a well-managed attachment relationship between the patient and the therapist that is neither too intense nor too detached. The patient suffering from this disorder is very sensitive to all forms of interpersonal contact. Because therapy involves interpersonal interaction, the therapist must be aware that it will inevitably provoke anxiety related to loss of a sense of self in the patient and that the resulting emotional experiences will threaten to overwhelm the patient's mental capacities, resulting in escalating emotions and inability to understand the motives of others accurately.

Psychologists and other mental health practitioners must be aware of this sensitivity as well if they are to prevent iatrogenic encounters with individuals who have a borderline personality disorder. Inpatient hospitalization, for example, is a highly emotional event for all patients and, if not handled properly, may exacerbate the symptoms of this disorder by overstimulating the attachment processes of those suffering from the disorder.

When unaltered intense therapies were given to patients, it is possible that they had poor long-term results due to the overstimulation during therapy. When it comes to regulating emotional responses and developing effective strategies for controlling their thoughts and feelings, patients with personality disorder are particularly vulnerable because for them it's difficult to think about their actions from subtle understandings of their thoughts and feelings. They seem to fall into what seems to be a sort of thoughtless condition, both in their interactions with others and in their interactions with themselves.

However, it soon becomes clear that the situation is more complex since these incapacities are not always visible, although perceptible at some moments. In contrast, during times of emotional distress, especially distress caused by real or potential loss, the ability to reason seems most vulnerable to seeming loss of mental capacity.

In light of the frequency and severity of this clinical issue within a public healthcare system, the challenge is how this knowledge and set of clinical observations may be effectively converted into a treatment strategy that may be beneficial. They are fundamental underlying techniques that may be utilized in the context of group and individual treatment.

10.4 Aims of Intervention in MBT

Interventions in this treatment are intended to accomplish certain goals. The first step is to increase control over emotional expression since it is impossible to examine internal representations without better control over the effect fully. Even though the reverse is also true, the identification and expression of effect are addressed first since they endanger treatment continuation and survival. Irrational emotion leads to impulsivity, and it is only after this effect has been brought under control that it is feasible to concentrate on internal representations and enhance the patient's sense of identity.

The goal of an intervention and the actual result of the intervention is more significant than the kind of intervention itself. The major goal of any intervention must be to restore mentalizing when it has been lost or to assist in maintaining it in situations when it is at risk of being lost or is already being lost. Any intervention that is successful in achieving these objectives may be utilized in this treatment. As a result, it takes a more lenient method to interventions than most other treatments, resulting in a greater variety of techniques available. This may account for its popularity and appeal to practitioners from a variety of schools, as well as the relatively short amount of training required before practitioners can begin using it in their everyday practice.

We do not need practitioners to learn a new treatment model from the ground up; rather, we urge that they adapt their existing practice to emphasize this method rather than on behaviors, cognitions, or insight. Our only requirement is that they take on a specific therapeutic stance and implement a series of steps to attempt to engage the patient in this process, beginning with some general psychotherapy methods such as compassion, assistance, and explanation, and then progressing to other interventions specifically designed to stress the attachment relationship within a controlled environment.

10.5 Therapeutic Stance

Mentalizing therapeutic stances should include the following characteristics:
• Humility stemming from an awareness of one's ignorance.
• Patience in identifying and accepting different perspectives.
• Legitimizing and accepting different perspectives.
• Actively questioning the patient about his or her experience, asking for detailed descriptions of experience (what questions) rather than explanations (why questions).

As a therapist, one of the essential aspects of this attitude is being aware of one's mentalizing shortcomings. In this context, it is critical to recognize that the therapist is always in danger of losing his or her ability to mentalize in the presence of a non-mentalizing patient, which should be recognized and avoided. Because of this, we see therapists' occasional enactments as a legitimate concomitant of the therapeutic relationship, something that needs to be acknowledged and acknowledged fully.

When mentalizing breakdowns occur, it is necessary to have the process rewound and the event examined, like with other instances of mentalizing breakdown. The two partners engaged in this collaborative patient-therapist relationship thus have a shared duty to comprehend the mental processes that underlie occurrences both inside and outside of treatment.

The mental representation of the Transference

I advise care while using transference interpretation in the treatment of personality disorder as it presupposes a degree of mentalizing ability on the part of the patient.

I caution practitioners about two things: first, the commonly stated goal of transference interpretation, which is to provide insight, and second, genetic aspects of transference interpretation, such as linking current experience to the past, because of the possibility of iatrogenic consequences.

Confirming the transference emotion, which entails establishing the patient's point of view, is the first stage. Of course, this does not imply that the therapist agrees with the patient's point of view, but it must be clear to the patient that the therapist has at the very least acknowledged his or her point of view.

When it comes to transference, the genetic method has the potential to invalidate the patient's experience. The second stage is to do research. It is necessary to determine the circumstances that resulted in the transference emotions. The behaviors associated with the thoughts or emotions must be identified and described explicitly, often in excruciating detail.

The third stage is accepting the therapist's simulation of the therapy session. The majority of the patient's sensations during the transference are likely to be based on reality, even if they have only a tenuous relationship to it. The majority of the time, this indicates that the therapist has been pulled into the transference and has behaved in a manner compatible with the patient's view of him or her. It may be tempting to blame the patient for the situation, but this would be counterproductive.

A more appropriate approach would be for the therapist to first openly recognize even partial enactments of the transference as unexplained voluntary acts for which he or she acknowledges agency and avoid labeling these activities as a distortion of the patient. The patient's ability to accept agency for involuntary actions and the fact that such acts do not contradict the overall attitude that the therapist is attempting to communicate may be especially important when drawing attention to such therapist components. It is only after that that distortions may be investigated.

The fourth step involves cooperation to arrive at an interpretation. Transference interpretations, like any other type of interpretive mentalizing, must be reached in the same spirit of cooperation as any other form of interpretive mentalizing. As part of our training, we instruct students to picture themselves seated next to the patient rather than on either side of them. They sit side by side, looking at the patient's thoughts and emotions and, where feasible, adopting the inquiring posture with one another.

The fifth stage is for the therapist to offer an alternate point of view, and the last step is to observe both the patient's and one's reactions.

I recommend that these stages be completed in order.

Therapists encourage patients to think about the relationship they are currently in, intending to focus their attention on another mind, the mind of the therapist, and assisting them in the task of contrasting their perception of themselves with how they are perceived by another, by the therapist or indeed by another person.

While we may draw parallels between patterns of relationships in therapy and patterns of relationships in childhood or currently outside of therapy, the goal is not to provide the patients with an explanation that they can use to control their behavior pattern, but rather to draw attention to one other puzzling phenomenon that necessitates thought and contemplation and is a part of our genetic makeup.

10.6 Effectiveness of MBT

It is a kind of long-term psychotherapy that uses mentalization to help people overcome their problems. It is defined as the capacity to think about one's thoughts. It assists us in making meaning of our ideas, beliefs, desires, and emotions, as well as connect them to our actions and behaviors. It is a natural ability that we all have and that we utilize in our daily lives. It serves as the foundation for all human interactions.

On the other hand, some individuals find it more difficult to prepare for some circumstances than others mentally. It is intended to enhance a person's ability to think mentally. We pay attention to what is going on in their thoughts and other people's minds, and we connect this information to comprehend better and relieve harmful behaviors.

Who is it intended for?

Mentalization-based treatment is appropriate for use with children, adolescents, and adults.

This treatment may be beneficial in the following situations:
• Depression
• Trauma

- Eating disorders

- Drug abuse and addiction

- Bipolar disorder with symptoms of mania.

- A variety of other personality problems.

Individuals experiencing long-term difficulties in their relationships and experiencing intense emotional distress and overwhelming feelings may find it particularly beneficial.

It is also beneficial for individuals who are wary of other people and have trouble interpreting the reactions of others to their questions and statements. Treatments based on mentalization may assist children, adolescents, and families who are experiencing psychological problems.

The duration of therapy

Each session lasts 60 minutes. Depending on the therapy program, group sessions may run anywhere from 75 to 90 minutes in length while treatment programs may last anywhere from 12 and 18 months.

Assessment

Throughout the evaluation process, two to four initial sessions with your therapist are required to fully understand your problems and determine the most suitable course of action. heHe'll look at how your problems have evolved, what is causing them to persist, and what therapies you have received so far. As part of the evaluation process, you will be asked to complete questionnaires that will assist you and your therapist track the success of your work together over time.

The individual, group, or a mix of these types of therapy sessions are available, depending on the evaluation outcome.

Sessions with a therapist

The goal of mentalization therapy sessions is to help you better understand yourself and others by focusing on the problems you are experiencing in your present life circumstances. You pay attention to what is going on in your mind while also considering what may be going on in the minds of others, which is especially important in circumstances that might result in strong emotional responses and harmful behavior. When you focus on understanding your own and other people's thoughts and feelings, it may assist you in better understanding and controlling your impulses, emotions, and behaviors enhancing interpersonal connections.

Advantages

Studies have indicated that mentally based therapy is a successful treatment for personality disorder, with symptom improvement persisting for years beyond the conclusion of the therapy program.

Research studies are now underway to see if it is also helpful in various other illnesses, including:
• Eating disorders
• Chronic depression
• Drug addiction
• Antisocial personality disorder

10.7 Risks and Adverse effects

When it comes to emotional issues, it may be tough to speak and think about them. You may be apprehensive about speaking in front of a group. As a result, some individuals may have worsening symptoms before seeing improvement. Therapists collaborate with you to help you cope with intense emotional responses, but this treatment is not for everyone, and it has its limitations.

During your evaluation, your therapist will speak to you about a variety of available alternative therapies.

Among the other psychological therapies are:
• Family therapy
• Group psychotherapy
• Cognitive-behavioral therapy
• Psychoanalytic psychotherapy
• Dialectical behavior treatment

Patients may benefit from the medicine, which may be given by a doctor or, in rare instances, by a member of the treatment team. In certain cases, patients may elect not to seek professional assistance for their condition and instead handle the situation themselves.

Conclusion

A borderline personality disorder is a severe mental disease characterized by an inability to properly regulate one's emotional responses. The disease manifests itself in the context of interpersonal relationships. Sometimes it affects all of them and other times it affects just one.

It typically starts throughout adolescence or the early stages of adolescence. Even though some people with this disorder have excellent functioning in specific situations, their private lives may be in disarray. Most individuals who have this disorder have difficulties controlling their emotions and thoughts, impulsive and often risky conduct and unstable relationships. Other disorders, such as depression, stress disorders, eating disorders, drug addiction, and other personality disorders, may often co-exist with this problem, as can other mental illnesses.

Diagnosis of a personality disorder is often overlooked, and it has been demonstrated that a misdiagnosis of this condition may delay or impede rehabilitation. Borderline personality, which involves both mood instability and manic episodes, is an example of a misdiagnosis. Although there are significant distinctions between the two diseases, they both entail unstable emotions in some form.

For a person suffering from mental illness, the mood swings may last for many weeks or even months and the associated episodes are considerably more frequent and may sometimes occur within a single day.

The study of the causes and risk factors for this personality disorder is still in its early phases. Scientists are largely in agreement that genetic and environmental factors are likely to be involved. Certain incidents that occurred throughout childhood, such as those involving emotional, physical, or sexual abuse, may also have affected the development of the condition. Loss, neglect, and bullying are all factors that may play a role in the disease.

Some individuals are more susceptible to developing this disorder than others because of their biology or genetics, and adverse childhood events may further raise the risk.

According to research, people with a personality disorder may have positive results, especially if they are actively involved in therapy. The majority of individuals who have borderline personality disorder feel that their symptoms are lessened and that their lives are better due to professional treatment. Even though not all symptoms may subside, there is often a significant reduction in problematic behaviors and suffering. Some symptoms may reappear while you are under stress. Individuals who have borderline personality disorder should return to treatment and other forms of assistance when this occurs.

Made in the USA
Columbia, SC
15 December 2021

51544859R00150